Caring for yo...
How to main...
& service yo...

Trevor Fry

D1429824

BOOK SOLD
NO LONGER R.H.P.L.
PROPERTY

RICHMOND HILL
PUBLIC LIBRARY

MAR 0 7 2013

RICHMOND GREEN
905-780-0711

Also from Veloce Publishing –
Caring for your car's bodywork and interior (Sahota)
Caring for your scooter – How to maintain & service your 49cc to 125cc twist & go
   scooter (Fry)
Electric Cars – The Future is Now! (Linde)
How your car works – Your guide to the components & systems of modern cars,
   including hybrid & electric vehicles (Linde)
Land Rover Series I-III – Your expert guide to common problems & how to fix them
   (Thurman)
Roads with a View – England's greatest views and how to find them by road
   (Corfield)
Roads with a View – Scotland's greatest views and how to find them by road
   (Corfield)
Roads with a View – Wales' greatest views and how to find them by road (Corfield)
The Efficient Driver's Handbook – Your guide to fuel efficient driving techniques and
   car choice (Moss)
Walking the dog – Motorway walks for drivers and dogs (Rees)

www.rac.co.uk
www.veloce.co.uk

This publication has been produced on behalf of RAC by Veloce Publishing Ltd.
The views and the opinions expressed by the author are entirely his own, and
do not necessarily reflect those of RAC. **Please do not undertake any of the
procedures described in this book unless you feel competent to do so, having
first read the full instructions.**

First published in October 2011 by Veloce Publishing Limited, Veloce House,
Parkway Farm Business Park, Middle Farm Way, Poundbury, Dorchester, Dorset,
DT1 3AR, England. ISBN: 978-1-845843-96-0 UPC: 6-36847-04396-4

Fax 01305 250479/e-mail info@veloce.co.uk
web www.veloce.co.uk or www.velocebooks.com.

All rights reserved. With the exception of quoting brief passages for
lication may be recorded, reproduced or transmitted by any means,
en permission of Veloce Publishing Ltd. Throughout this book logos,
been used for the purposes of identification, illustration and decoration.
mark holder as this is not an official publication.
iervices. The RAC logo is the registered trade mark of RAC Motoring

or books on other transport or related hobby subjects, are invited to
lishing at the above address.

)ata – A catalogue record for this book is available from the British

by Veloce Publishing Ltd on Apple Mac.

**RICHMOND HILL
PUBLIC LIBRARY**

MAR 0 7 2013

**RICHMOND GREEN
905-780-0711**

Caring for your car
How to maintain & service your car

Trevor Fry

Contents

Introduction

Who the book is for

This book is for anyone who wants to carry out basic maintenance on their car and gain a bit of knowledge at the same time.

Somebody who doesn't want to spend time going through a highly technical manual, and probably getting lost in the process, just to find out how to check the oil level!

Why buy this book?

It's written in plain English and illustrated with full colour photographs.

The work is carried out with the most basic of tool sets, and not only will you have the satisfaction of doing the job yourself, but you'll have learnt something on the way.

This book is not a full-blown, 'take-off every nut and bolt' manual. It covers the basic servicing and maintenance needed to keep your car safe and on the road. Doing your first oil change should save you the cost of the book, or more!

What's covered

Fluid levels and topping up
Brakes: disc, drum, and bleeding
CV boots
Filters: air and oil
Tyres
Sparkplugs
Bulbs and fuses
Wheel bearing adjustment
Wipers
Windscreen checks
Safety checks

What's not covered

Serious mechanical repairs

Thanks

The author wishes to thank Bosch for supplying the sparkplug information, and Unipart for making available new parts for him to photograph.

6

Important information

- If anything contained in this book contradicts what's written in the vehicle manufacturer's handbook (referred to as 'handbook' throughout this book), the official handbook will *always* take priority.
- The guidance in this book is general, so, whilst your car and its individual components may look a little different from the featured project cars and their components, the actions described will still be performed in essentially the same manner.
- Where general terms, such as oil, grease, coolant, etc, are used, always be sure that you are using the correct type for your car. Consult the handbook, and seek professional advice if you are in any doubt.
- All bolts, nuts and screws are turned **anti-clockwise to undo,** unless stated otherwise in the handbook.
- Inhaled dust from brake shoes and pads can be harmful to health, so wear a face mask when working on the brakes. It's also a good idea to wash the brake assembly with water or proprietary brake cleaner before stripping it, to keep the dust down.
- Always use the correct size tools (spanners, sockets, screwdrivers, etc) or you risk rounding off nuts and the heads of bolts, or stripping the slots out of screws. Also, you increase the risk of injuring yourself if the tool slips when you're applying pressure.
- When doing any maintenance always turn off the ignition and remove the key.
- Before attempting any form of maintenance ensure you can work in safety, that you have the required tools, enough room and ample lighting, and, most importantly, you know how you are going to do the task and that you are competent. If in any doubt, *always* seek professional advice.
- To jack up your car always follow the procedure beginning on page 14.

Your vehicle details

Make/model	
Registration	
Engine number	
Oil type/capacity	
Sparkplug number	
Tyre size/pressure	
Front	
Rear	
Insurance renewal date	
MoT renewal date	
Road tax renewal date	

Items to familiarise yourself with

It's recommended that you familiarise yourself with the positions of the following, all of which are normally found in the engine compartment:

Note: You **may** find the terms shown in capitals in the picture captions marked on the body, lid or cap of items in the engine bay (Figs 1 to 6a).

Fig 2. Brake fluid reservoir (for topping up brake fluid) 'BRAKE FLUID.'

Fig 1. Coolant reservoir (for topping up the engine's coolant) 'COOLANT.'

Fig 3. Washer bottle (fluid for washing the windscreen) 'WASHERS' or the wiper symbol.

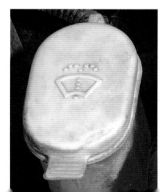

Fig 4. Typical canister-type oil filter (in this case low down and at the rear of the engine).

Fig 5. Power steering fluid reservoir (for topping up power steering fluid) 'POWER STEERING.'

Fig 4a. Typical canister-type oil filter (this one's at the front of the engine).

Fig 6. The oil filler cap. Engine oil is added here. 'OIL' (may be coloured yellow and/or depict an oil can).

Fig 6a. The oil filler cap (arrowed) is located on the rocker box cover/cam cover at the top of the engine.

Weekly checks

Lights
All lights should be in working order, so check the following:
Headlights on high beam
Headlights on low beam
Sidelights
Rear lights, including poor visibility light/s ('foglights')
Stoplights (these are best checked by backing up to a garage door or other partly reflective surface)
Turn indicators
Reversing lights

Note: In cold weather the heat created by the bulbs helps to establish a film of dry dirt on the light lenses, which causes a decrease in intensity. Ensure that lenses are kept clean.

Check engine oil level
Figs 6 to 8. With the engine cold and the car on level ground, use the dipstick to check the engine oil level. The oil level should be between the minimum and maximum markers (Fig 8). If the level is low, top up with suitable engine oil (see handbook). Do not over fill. If there is evidence of an oil leak, find the source

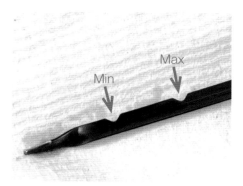

Fig 8. Dipstick end showing minimum and maximum markers.

of the leak and have it repaired before driving any significant distance.

Screen washer level & wipers (front & back)
Figs 3 & 11. The screen wash reservoir in the engine bay has markers on it to indicate the level of screen wash. If it runs out, the windscreen can't be cleaned effectively. The level can be topped up with clean water and/or screen wash and you can fill the reservoir right to the top.

Pull the wiper blades away from the windscreen and check for splits and

Fig 7. Oil dipstick (for measuring engine oil level). It may be coloured yellow.

Fig 9. Topping up windscreen washer reservoir.

tears along the leading edge of the wiper blades, and for signs of wear where the blade attaches to the main rubber; also that the blades are held against the windscreen by a decent amount of tension. **Caution!** Faulty wiper blades should be replaced as a matter of urgency. New arms will restore correct tension to the wiper blades.

Brake fluid

Fig 10. Doesn't normally require topping up. The level only lowers as the pads gradually wear (there's not normally any discernible fluid displacement with brake shoe wear).

The minimum and maximum levels are marked on the exterior of the reservoir. **Caution!** Do not drive with the level below the minimum.

Consult the handbook for the correct grade of brake fluid.

If the brake fluid level does fall significantly, check the brake system for leaks, or for excessively worn brake pads.

Fig 10. Topping up brake fluid reservoir.

Fig 11. Topping up coolant reservoir.

Coolant

Caution! Do not top up when the engine is hot – there's a severe risk of scalding!

The coolant reservoir will have the minimum and maximum levels marked on its body. **Caution!** On no account run the engine until the coolant level is above minimum.

Fig 11. The coolant reservoir can be topped up with water alone, but it's not advisable as this does not protect the engine from internal corrosion or the coolant from freezing. **Caution!** If you do top up with water alone, it's essential that you get the strength of antifreeze/inhibitor checked before the onset of winter. You can purchase antifreeze (specific gravity) testing kits at most car accessory shops.

The handbook will tell you what proportion of antifreeze/inhibitor and water should be mixed before topping up the coolant reservoir, it's usually around 25 per cent antifreeze/inhibitor to 75 per cent water.

Tyres (tires)

If a tyre is flat or partially deflated, pump it up to the correct pressure (see handbook) and check it again after 30 minutes. If you think it is losing pressure, get it checked at a garage or tyre centre in case it has a faulty valve or a puncture.

If the tyre tread is low – less than 1.6mm (the UK legal limit) – or has damaged walls, cuts, bulges, etc, it's unsafe and should be replaced.

Power steering fluid level

Fig 5. This doesn't usually need topping up, unless there's a leak.

The power steering tank may have the minimum and maximum levels marked on the outside, or a mini-dipstick fitted inside the reservoir cap.

Power steering uses a special hydraulic fluid: consult the handbook.

Caution! Do not allow the fluid level to fall below the minimum marker.

Caution! Do not attempt to drive the car with faulty power steering – the steering will be very heavy!

Automatic Transmission Fluid (ATF)

ATF is used in an automatic gearbox. There may be a dipstick for you to check the ATF fluid level, although many modern cars have a sealed gearbox requiring no maintenance or manufacturer dealer attention only.

If your car has an ATF dipstick to check fluid level, it will be in the engine compartment, and be of similar appearance to the engine oil dipstick, but the top may be coloured red or blue.

There are so many different automatic gearboxes, and so many different procedures for checking and topping up the ATF fluid, that it's impossible to give reliable general information. Also, there are different

types of automatic transmission fluid and care must be taken to top up with ATF to the correct specification. It's recommended you consult the handbook to find the correct procedure for checking and topping up ATF level.

If no mention can be found in the handbook, or you are unsure of how to proceed after reading what information you have found, then please seek guidance from a garage/service centre.

Gearbox & differential oil levels

It's unusual for the oil levels in the gearbox and differential unit to drop unless a leaking seal is allowing oil to escape (evidenced by regular oil stains on the ground beneath your car and indicating the need for a repair, which is beyond the scope of this book).

As the car must be level, access to the oil level/filler plug/hole is very difficult without a ramp to lift the whole car or an inspection pit. Therefore, it's recommended that you take you car to a garage once a year to have the oil levels in the gearbox and differential checked.

Warning lights

This section lists the most common warning lights seen on the dashboard, but is not an exhaustive list. If you are unsure, refer to the vehicle manufacturer's handbook for further information.

Battery (also known as ignition light)

Indicates that the ignition is turned on, and also the battery power before the engine is started. The light should go out when the engine is running.

If the light flickers when the engine is running – at a higher speed than

Fig 12. Battery indicator.

Fig 15. Handbrake indicator.

Fig 13. Oil indicator.

Fig 16. ABS indicator.

Fig 14. STOP indicator.

Fig 17. Engine indicator.

and should go off when the engine is running. **Note:** This light indicates oil pressure, although it may also indicate low oil, so you are advised to check the oil level with the car's dipstick. If the oil level is okay, you need to have the oil pressure checked at a garage.

ABS

Lit when the ignition is turned on, it should go off when the engine is running. If the light remains on when the engine is running, this indicates a fault with the ABS, in which case get your car checked by a garage.

STOP

This may be lit when the ignition is turned on, but should go out after a few seconds. **Caution!** If this warning light stays on, there may be a serious problem with the engine, and you should stop and turn it off immediately.

Note: The cause can be something as easy to rectify as low coolant level, so check the liquid levels first.

Engine symbol (onboard diagnostic symbol)

This will light up when the ignition is turned on, and should go off after a few seconds. If the light remains on, it generally indicates an engine/emissions problem or that the car requires a service.

Note: If your car has a digital odometer the manufacturer may have programmed it to also display faults as soon as the ignition is turned on – like low oil level, etc. After a few seconds it returns to displaying the vehicle mileage.

tickover – there could be a fault with the charging system or the alternator drivebelt is slipping. If the battery light fails to come on when the ignition is turned on, the battery may be fully discharged ('flat'), there may be a bad battery connection or, perhaps, a fuse has blown.

Handbrake/brake pads

Indicates that the handbrake is on or, if the light is on when the handbrake is off, the brake pads may be worn. If the light flickers when the car is driven it usually also means the pads are worn. If the pads are okay, check the wire coming from the pad; its insulation can wear through and cause a short, causing the light to flicker.

Oil light

This is lit when the ignition is turned on

Recommended tools

Socket set (4mm-32mm)
Selection of spanners (6mm-22mm)

Correct size sparkplug spanner
Torque wrench*
Vice grip pliers
Allen keys
Selection of screwdrivers (both flat and cross blade)
Pliers
G-clamp (small)
Insulation tape
Feeler gauge
Wire brush
Selection of graded wet-and-dry abrasive paper
Axle stands and/or car ramps
Trolley jack or car manufacturer's jack
Wheel chocks
Tyre pressure gauge
Tyre tread depth gauge
Small voltmeter or multimeter

* The correct torque settings for various components can usually be found on the web. Put your car's make and model followed by 'torque settings' into a search engine and then hit 'search.'

Extras (to make things easier for you)
Oil filter removal tool
Brake calliper piston reset tool
One-person brake bleed kit

Also recommended
A large piece of cardboard to push screws/bolts into, or to lay out removed items on. This will prevent parts from getting lost. You can then label all the parts and record their positions so that you can put them back where they came from; also in the reverse order to which they were removed.

A mobile phone with camera/digital camera means you can take pictures of an assembly before dismantling it (so you can see how it looks complete). This will help during reassembly, particularly if you take pictures from different angles.

Using a jack

Note: Where this book instructs you to jack up your car, or lower it, always follow the procedure and advice below.

Caution! Ensure you are working in a safe and level environment. And remember, a jack is for lifting, an axle stand is for supporting.

• With the engine turned off, ensure the handbrake is fully-applied.
• Chock the wheels you won't be raising (ie: the rear wheels if you are lifting the front wheel/s) with wooden wedges or blocks to stop the car rolling backwards or forwards.

Fig 18. Front wheels chocked.

• Select first or reverse gear ('Park' for automatics) to help prevent the car rolling if you are lifting either the front wheel/s on a rear-wheel drive car or the rear wheel/s on a front-wheel drive car.
• If you plan to remove a wheel or wheels once the car is jacked, now is a good time to remove the wheel hub trim (if fitted) to reveal the wheel nuts/ bolts. The trim is generally a tension fit, and can be prised off gently using a screwdriver (Fig 19).
Loosen the wheel nuts/bolts just half a turn each while the tyres are all still in contact with the ground.
• Next, jack up the car using the car manufacturer's supplied jack, which is

Fig 19. Removing the wheel trim from the centre of a wheel.

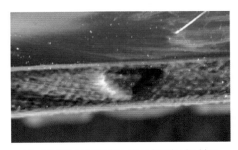

Fig 20. Sill indentation showing the jacking position under sill.

Fig 21. Sill cut-out showing the jacking position.

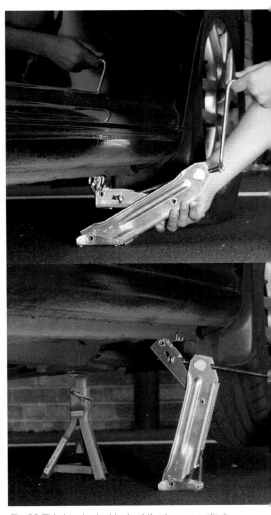

Fig 22 This is a typical jack of the type supplied with the car. Engage the jack in the correct position under the sill (rocker) – see Figs 20 & 21. Then wind the handle to lift the relevant wheel from the ground. Note axle stand added for security.

designed to locate correctly with the recommended jacking points.

If you do not have the original jack, use another type; placing it under a strong point in the car's underframe (using a wood or rubber packing piece to protect the chassis rails from the jack's lifting pad) (Figs 25 & 26).

15

Do not attempt to jack the car with the jack positioned under a sill (rocker), unless there's an indicated jacking point that the jack fits (often indicated by a cut-out in the seam of the sill or an indentation in the sill itself (Figs 20 & 21).

• With the car at the correct working height (ie: with the tyre just off the ground), support it further with an axle stand (Fig 24). If you are using an axle stand for support, you'll need to use the jack to raise the car enough to position the stand beneath a strong point, then slowly lower the car onto the stand.)

If you wish to work on both sides of the car in the same session, and you have an extra jack and an extra axle stand, you can also jack the opposite wheel at this

Fig 23 Another typical jack of the type supplied with the car. Engage the jack in the correct position under the sill (rocker) – see Figs 20 & 21. Then wind the handle to lift the relevant wheel from the ground. Note axle stand added for security.

Fig 24. Vehicle jacked up beneath the 'chassis' with an axle stand providing secondary support.

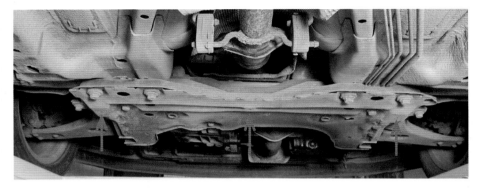

Fig 25 & 26. Typical underbody of a modern car. Strong points like those arrowed can be used to jack the car, but do interpose a block of wood between the jack pad and the lifting point to protect the car's frame from damage. NEVER work under a car supported by jacks alone, or one without chocked wheels: if it falls on you, it will kill you! **Caution!** Do not jack under the floorpan; always use a strong point.

point, following the same procedure. **Caution!** Do not work on the car when it's supported only by one jack; always use a strong and secure secondary support for your own safety and make sure the wheels remaining on the ground are firmly chocked.

• With the car jacked and supported safely, you can now fully undo the wheel nuts/bolts you loosened earlier and remove the raised wheel/s.

• When you've finished working on the car, replace the wheel and tighten the wheel nuts/bolts.

• With the car supported by the jack, remove the axle stand and use the jack to lower the car slowly to the ground.

• Fully tighten the wheel nuts/bolts now that all the tyres are on the ground.

• Replace the wheel trim (if fitted), ensuring it's clipped in all the way round the edges.

• Recheck the tightness of all nuts/bolts after a short trip.

one

Tyres, wheels, brakes, steering & suspension – inspection

This chapter covers inspection of the tyres, wheels, brakes steering and suspension. Solutions to any problems you discover here can be found in the next chapter on maintenance.

Unless clearly stated, the following information and procedures are applicable to both the front and rear of the car.

Tyres (tires)

Examine the tyres for:
• Bulges (where the actual tyre wall components have separated).
• Splits or cuts in the tyre wall.
• Fig 30 & 31. Depth of tread (by looking at the tread depth indicators moulded into the tyre tread or using a depth gauge).
• Foreign objects embedded in the tread.

If the tread is excessively worn in the centre or the two outer edges,
the probable cause is incorrect tyre pressure. If the tread is excessively worn on one outer edge, there could be a tracking error – have the tracking checked by a garage.

Tyre pressure

There are two types of tyre pressure gauge you can use to check tyre pressures:

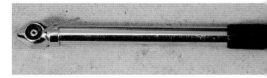

Fig 27. Analogue tyre pressure gauge. The opening with the rubber seal (arrowed) is pressed onto the valve in the wheel rim.

Analogue pressure gauge

• Using an analogue gauge similar to that in Fig 27, remove the black cap from the end to allow the gauge to extend when pressure reading is taken.

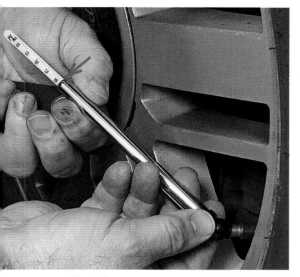

Fig 28.Tyre pressure reading (arrowed).

• Remove the dust cap from the valve in the rim of the wheel.
• Ensure the extension is fully into the gauge and push the gauge onto the valve, as in Fig 28.
• Allow the gauge to extend.
• Remove it from the valve and read the tyre pressure at the point that the extension exits the body of the gauge.
• Refit the valve cap.

Digital pressure gauge
• Using a digital pressure gauge similar to that in Fig 29, remove the dust cap from wheel valve.
• Push the gauge onto the valve, as shown.
• Read the pressure shown on the display screen.
• Remove the gauge and refit the valve cap.

Fig 29. Using a digital pressure gauge to check tyre pressure. The figure is shown on the display, here in psi.

Tread depth
Use a tread depth tool (Fig 31). Allow the probe end to extend into the tread groove, and read the depth from the other end where the gauge exits the body of the tool.

Fig 30. Tread depth indicator (arrowed) moulded into the tyre.

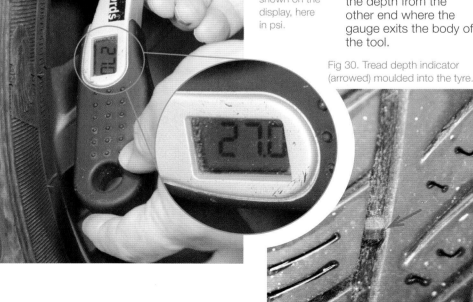

Fig 31. Typical tyre tread depth gauge.

The remaining checks require the car to be jacked off the ground. Jack up the car now, following the 'Using a jack' procedure detailed at the start of this book, but do not remove the wheel/s until you have completed the first check for wheel bearing play.

Wheel bearings

It's easiest to check for wheel bearing play before the wheel is removed: Fig 32. Facing the side of the wheel, hold it in the quarter-to-three position and try to rock the wheel in and out – there shouldn't be any discernible 'play' (free movement). Play will be heard as a slight click/knock when the wheel is rocked.

Note: When checking the front wheel bearings, you are gently feeling for play at the hub, not trying to turn the wheel and the hub together.

Now undo and remove the wheel nuts/bolts (you'll need someone to apply the brakes to prevent the wheel rotating) and remove the wheel. If there's grease leaking from around the domed cover in the centre of the wheel (Fig 33) it has either been incorrectly fitted or needs to be renewed.

Fig 33. Dome cover in the centre of the wheel.

With the wheel/s removed, you now have access to the brake pipe, brake calliper and disc or drum.

The author finds it easier to work to an 'outside in' routine; that is the examination of the items as they are removed, so that you can Double-check each item as you refit it.

Fig 32. Checking for play in the wheel bearing.

Wheels

Look for cracks in the wheel itself, and for damage around the rim where the tyre meets the wheel (Fig 34), normally caused by hitting the kerb when parking.

Fig 34. This wheel should be replaced.

Fig 35. Pad inspection slot in the rear of the calliper.

Brake pads

With the wheel removed, brake pads can be viewed in situ by looking through the slot in the calliper (Fig 35). If checking the front pads, you can turn the hub to make this easier.

The disc is in the middle, with a pad each side, and then the pad backing plates.

Depending on the make and model of car/pad, the pads could have a distinctive groove through

Fig 36. New (left) and old pads (note that the new pads may have a wear indicator slot: when this is no longer visible the pads must be renewed).

21

the centre, which, if visible, can help to assess wear.

Some cars have brake pad wear warning indicators that display on the dashboard when the brake pads are getting thin. However, you should still carry out visual checks on the pads, as these indicators can sometimes be unreliable due to bad electrical connections.

Caution! Do not refit any pad with less than 5mm/³⁄₁₆in of pad depth (Fig 36).

Brake discs

Look for extreme wear (Fig 37) on both sides of the disc; normally indicated by a large ridge at the outer and inner edges of the pad contact surface of the disc. Also look for deep gouges or cracks in the disc.

Fig 37. Close-up of a brake disc in situ showing wear ridges.

Brake drums

(Fig 38). Check the exterior of the drum for cracks. Also look for oil or brake fluid that appears to be coming from inside the drum, as this could indicate a leaking brake cylinder or a leaking hub seal.

Fig 38. Typical drum brake with central domed cover.

Brake hoses

Fig 39 & 40. Check that both ends of the hose are secure: where it connects to the solid brake pipe on the car body

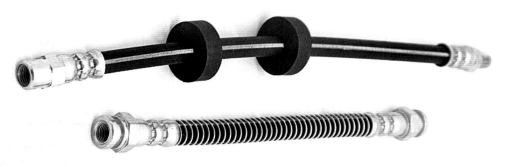

Fig 39. Different types of brake hose.

Fig 40. Typical brake hose connecting the brake pipe and calliper and other brake components.

and where the hose connects to the brake calliper. Examine the brake hose itself for signs of wear, leakage, or cracking. This can be done by flexing the hose in different directions and visually checking to ensure there are no cracks where the hose is bent or stressed. Any damage means the hose must be renewed.

Suspension

Figs 41 to 43. Look for a cracked or broken coil spring, and oil leaking

Fig 41. Typical front suspension (strut type). It may look different on your car, but will still consist of a strut, spring, and an hydraulic damper.

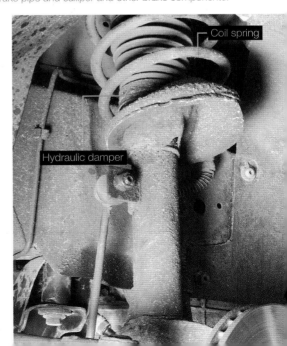

Fig 43. Typical rear spring.

from the hydraulic damper. A sure sign of oil leaking is if the dirt on the unit is deep black in colour and looks wet.

CV (constant velocity) joint and boot

Fig 44. This is the joint at the back of the hub assembly that transmits drive to the wheel. The joint is enclosed in a protective rubber boot/gaiter.

Examine the whole boot (rotating the wheel hub if necessary) for cracks, cuts or rips. If there's oil or grease on the outside of the boot, then the boot has almost certainly failed and should be renewed. Dirt entering the CV joint can quickly cause serious damage, making it necessary to renew the joint – not a cheap option!

Fig 42. Typical rear damper/shock absorber (the arrow indicates the main area to check for oil leaks).

Fig 44. Typical CV (constant velocity) joint boot (gaiter).

Note: An indication of a dry (insufficiently lubricated) CV joint – and probable CV boot failure – is a loud clicking when turning the car with the steering on full lock. This normally means the boot or joint needs immediate attention.

Trackrod (steering arm)

Fig 45. Check for excess play in the ball joints, which can be felt and may be heard as a knock when pulling or pushing the steering arm. Also check that the arm itself is not obviously bent, and that the rubber boots over the joints aren't torn or split.

Suspension ball joint/s

Fig 46. This is the joint that the wheel and hub assembly turn on when the steering is turned. Check for play in the joint by pulling and pushing the hub forwards and backwards. Also examine the rubber boot for tears.

If your car has double wishbone suspension, there will also be a top ball joint (Fig 47).

Track rod

Ball joint

Rubber boot

Fig 45. Typical track rod ball joint to the wheel hub carrier/upright.

Fig 46. Typical bottom ball joint (arrowed).

Fig 47. Typical double wishbone suspension with ball joints at top and bottom of the upright which carries the stub axle.

Anti-roll bar

Fig 48. This bar connects the suspension on one side of the car to the suspension on the other side to prevent excessive body roll. It will have rubber/nylon-bushed mountings on the car's subframe, as well as link arms and joints connecting it to the suspension. You need to check all the mountings for security and the bushes and joints for signs of excessive wear/play.

Fig 48. One end of a typical anti-roll bar (it is connected to the car's frame and the suspension).

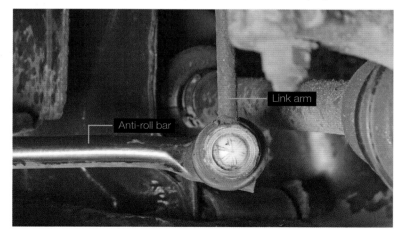

two

Tyres, wheels, brakes, steering & suspension – maintenance

This chapter describes how to solve any problems you may have identified during the inspection procedure in chapter one.

Information specific to the front or the rear of the car is clearly identified.

Caution! Any faults with the suspension, trackrods, suspension ball joints, or anti-roll bar should be rectified by a professional immediately, and are beyond the scope of this book.

Tyres (tires)

Points to consider:
• Bulges in the tyre wall indicate the separation of the tyre's internal elements, making the tyre unsafe and illegal.
• Tears in the tyre wall, or serious cuts in the tyre tread require the tyre to be replaced.
• If foreign items are found embedded in the tread, leave them, as they may

be sealing a leak. It also means you can drive (carefully!) to the nearest garage and get the tyre checked. You should do this straightaway, as the tyre may need to be renewed, if not repairable.
• Severely worn tyres, or tyres on which the 'canvas' beneath the tread can be seen (no matter how small an area), are unsafe and must be replaced.

At the time of writing, in the UK a

Fig 49. Tread is worn level with the top of a wear indicator: this tyre should be replaced.

tyre is considered unsafe and illegal if there's less than 1.6mm depth of tread in a continuous band around the tyre circumference and across the central three-quarters of the tread width.

Wheels

If a pressed steel wheel rim is damaged, a tyre fitting garage may be able to reset the rim correctly. It's very important for it to be correctly set, as this helps create and maintain the seal between the wheel and the tyre. If the wheel rim cannot be reset, the wheel will need to be renewed.

Damaged alloy wheels will need to be repaired by a wheel specialist.

Wheel bearing play

Identifying type of wheel bearing

If your car is all-wheel drive, the wheel bearings are not adjustable and will need replacing if worn, a procedure beyond the scope of this book.

If your car is rear-wheel drive, it's probable that there are what are known as taper roller bearings on the front stub axles. And if your car is front-wheel drive, it's likely there are taper roller bearings in the rear hubs.

Taper roller bearings can be adjusted to compensate for wear. Front or back, the adjustment procedure is the same.

Removing play from taper bearings
Required
Jack/s
Axle stands (jack stands)
Screwdrivers
Socket set
Wheel bearing grease
Soft hammer
Pliers

• Jack up the car (page 14) and remove the wheel to reveal the brake drum or disc (depending on the type of brake).

The bearing nut is located in the centre of the wheel, often covered by either a flat disc or a domed dust cap.
• Fig 50. Using a small, flat-bladed screwdriver, gently lever out the domed/flat cover to allow access to the stub axle nut.

Fig 50. Removing a typical domed cover.

• You'll now be looking at a nut on the stub axle with which the taper bearings can be adjusted. Fig 51 shows a hub 'nut' that looks as though it has a cover on it, but it hasn't. In fact, it's a set of four nuts permanently located inside a sealed holder, although it should be treated as an ordinary nut. **Caution!** On no account should you try to disassemble the hub nut.

Alternatively, you may find a staked nut (Fig 52). If so, use a small screwdriver or punch to completely lift the stake out of the groove to free the nut.
• If you think the bearing may be dry of grease, remove the nut completely. Also remove the large washer to give access to the outer part of the bearing.
• If you find the bearing is dry, but

Fig 51. Infintely adjustable self-locking bearing 'nut' (actually a number of nuts within a cage).

Fig 53. Taper roller bearing and bearing housing.

Fig 52. Infintely adjustable bearing nut with a soft collar which can be staked into a groove in the stub axle to lock it in position.

otherwise clean, remove the outer roller bearing (Fig 53) and apply a thin layer of new wheel bearing grease to all accessible bearing surfaces.

If the outer part of the bearing doesn't come out with the washer, it can either be pulled off with the brake drum (if the brake drum is secured by the same fitting), or the outer part of the bearing can normally be knocked out by tapping the back of the drum (not the backplate) or brake calliper with a soft-faced hammer.

Note: Be careful not to let the outer bearing drop on the ground.

• You can now also spread a thin layer of grease over all the roller surfaces, remembering to put some grease on the inner bearing rollers.
• When finished, replace the outer bearing, followed by the cleaned washer and nut.
• Use a torque wrench to tighten the bearing nut to the correct setting. Over-tightness or looseness will cause excessive wear on the bearing, and could lead to premature failure.
• **Caution!** Remember to re-stake the nut (Fig 52), if applicable.
• Refit the domed cover and give it a light tap in the middle to set it – this cover is a tension fit, so you do not have to hammer it in!

Renewing brake pads

Caution! When fitting new brake pads always fit them to both sides of the car at the same time.

Be careful not to contaminate the pad faces with dirt or grease from your hands.

Required
Jack/s
Axle stands (jack stands)
New pads
Spanners
Socket set
Torque wrench
G-clamp (front only)
Piston spreader (front only)
Piston reset tool (rear only), if applicable

FRONT

Removing old brake pads

• Using spanners, or a socket and spanner, undo the lower, outer bolt on the back of the calliper (Fig 57).
• With this bolt removed, pivot the outer part of the calliper upward on the top mounting bolt to allow access to the brake pads, taking care not to put a strain on the brake hose (Fig 58).
• Disconnect the wire for the brake pad wear indicator (if fitted), and remove the brake pads by sliding them out of the calliper. If they're a tight fit, you can tap them out gently with a soft-faced hammer. **Note:** There may be

anti-squeal shims fitted. These look like small metal plates and fit between the backs of the brake pads and the calliper to prevent squealing noises. The shims

Fig 55. Side of a typical calliper.

Fig 54. Different but nevertheless typical brake pads.

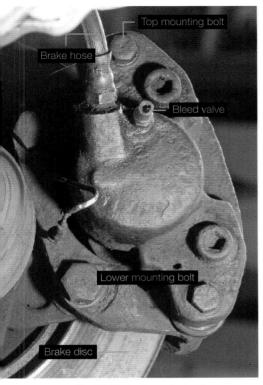

Fig 56. Back of a typical calliper.

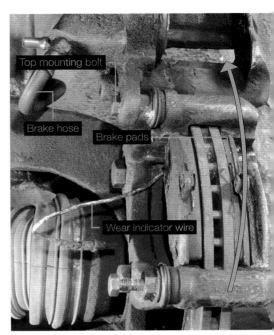

Fig 58. This typical calliper pivots upward, to reveal the brake pads.

Fig 57. Undoing the lower bolt.

Fig 59. Empty calliper; pads removed.

31

will also need to be removed, and then refitted behind the new brake pads.

• Using a proprietary brake cleaning fluid and clean rag, wipe clean the visible surface of the protruding calliper piston, and check for corrosion/damage on the piston's surface. **Caution!** If corrosion or damage is evident, refit the old pads and take the car to a garage for professional attention, as these faults could cause brake failure.

Preparing to install new brake pads

To accommodate the new thicker pads, the calliper piston needs to be pushed back into its housing. Use a brake calliper piston spreader tool (Fig 60) or an old brake pad and a medium-sized G-clamp to push the piston back.

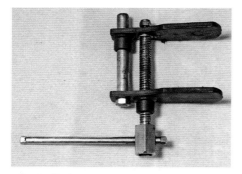

Fig 60. Typical brake calliper piston spreader.

Sometimes the calliper needs to be removed from the hub so that the piston is not hidden behind the brake disc. This may simply involve undoing only one calliper mounting bolt, loosening the other, and then pivoting the calliper unit away from the disc, but this is dependent on the amount of movement allowed by the brake hose. **Caution!** On no account put stress on this hose.

If you do need to undo both mounting bolts, do not allow the calliper to hang by the brake hose, instead suspend it on a piece of wire or string.

• Next set up the calliper as if you were going to bleed it (Fig 68) as you'll need to open the bleed nipple half a turn as the piston is retracted, so that displaced fluid collects in a jar without allowing air to enter the system. If the tube does not have a one-way valve it is essential that outlet end of the tube remains immersed in the fluid in the jar while the bleed nipple is open. **Caution!** Don't forget to close the bleed nipple when the piston is fully retracted.

Using a piston spreader

• Insert the piston spreader tool into the calliper with one plate each side of the disc (ie: one plate against the piston and the other against the inside of the outer part of the calliper).

• Turn the handle clockwise, pushing the calliper piston and calliper outer apart, until the piston is pushed back flush with its housing.

Using a G-clamp

• Place the G-clamp over the calliper with the fixed side of the clamp behind the piston housing and the adjustable side against the backing plate of an old pad sandwiched between it and the face of the piston (to prevent damaging the piston face).

• Slowly close the clamp to push the piston back into the housing, until the piston is flush with it.

• With the piston pushed back, remove the spreader/clamp and ensure the piston face is clean, and that it shows no signs of fluid leaking around the seal between the piston and housing.

• If applicable, refit the calliper assembly to the suspension upright by installing the two large bolts. **Caution!** These bolts need to be secure, so it's recommended that you apply thread locking fluid (such as Loctite) to their threads and tighten them as much as you can by hand using a half inch drive socket and the standard T-bar from the socket set. If you have a torque wrench, you should be able to find the correct setting by doing a web search.

Installing new brake pads
• With the piston fully back into its housing, check that all is clean and undamaged, then spread a **thin** smear of copper grease over the **back** (the metal part) of both new brake pads – **Caution!** Don't contaminate the pad friction material faces.
• If one of the new brake pads has a wear indicator wire fitted, this pad must be fitted closest to the piston. Insert the new brake pads into the brake calliper with the friction material sides facing the brake disc (Fig 61). Refit the anti-squeal shims (if applicable).

Fig 61. New brake pads (arrowed) in place. Note copper grease on pad backplate.

The pads are meant to be a friction fit (ie not too loose, but tight enough to hold them) in the calliper. If you cannot get them fully home, gently tap the edge of the pad backing plates with a soft-faced hammer. If you find they do not go in relatively easily when tapping them, remove and check the edges of the pads and the calliper guides for roughness. This problem can usually be solved by running a piece of 800 wet-and-dry paper along the edge of the pad to remove any unevenness in the coat of paint, and/or running it along the pad channel in the calliper to remove any corrosion.
• With the new brake pads slid into position, bring the outer part of the calliper back down over the pads, ensuring not to trap the wear indicator cable (if fitted). You may need to push the outer part of the calliper in quite hard, as it sits against the brake pad securing springs (if fitted).
• Replace and fully tighten the lower calliper bolt using spanners or a socket and spanner.

Fig 62. Here, the calliper body is closed. The brake pad wear indicator wire (arrowed) coming from the pad is redundant in this particular application, and so can be snipped off.

• Reconnect the wear indicator wire. If this electrical cable is not required in your application, it can be snipped off (Fig 62).

• Check the fluid level in the brake reservoir and pump the brake pedal to bring the new pads into contact with the disc/s.

• Brake bleeding is recommended (see chapter 3) to ensure the brake is purged of air. **Caution!** Bleeding is essential if there is any change to brake pedal 'feel' (ie: sponginess) or it travels further.

• Double-check everything then refit the road wheel/s and lower the car to the ground.

• Retighten the wheel nuts/bolts and take the car for a short drive.

Caution! You may find that the brakes are initially less responsive, due to the pads being new. They will take approximately 200 miles to bed in fully.

REAR

The method for replacing rear brake pads differs slightly to that for the front brakes, mainly because of the parking brake adjustment feature built into the rear callipers, which means the calliper pistons have to be retracted by a different method.

Removing old brake pads

• With the car safely jacked and the

Fig 63. Undoing the lower bolt.

road wheel/s removed, release the handbrake. **Note:** Do not operate the handbrake whilst the rear brakes are disassembled.

• Using spanners, or a socket and spanner, undo the lower bolt (Fig 63) on the inside of the outer calliper, followed by the upper bolt (Fig 64).

• Remove the outer part of the calliper (Fig 65).

• Remove the brake pads by sliding them out of the main calliper housing. If they're a tight fit, you can gently tap them out with a soft-faced hammer.

• Using a proprietary brake cleaning

Fig 64. Undoing the upper bolt.

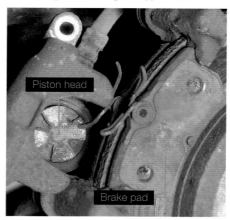

Piston head

Brake pad

Fig 65. Here, the outer part of a rear brake calliper has been removed to reveal the brake pads and the piston head, which has indentations on its surface for the resetting tool.

fluid and clean rag, wipe clean the visible surface of the protruding calliper piston, and check for corrosion/damage on the piston's surface. **Caution!** If corrosion or damage is evident, refit the old pads and take the car to a garage for professional attention, as these faults could cause brake failure.

Preparing to install new brake pads

• The calliper piston needs to be pushed back into its housing so that the new, thicker brake pads can be accommodated. This is usually done using a piston reset tool, like the one shown in Fig 66. However, some cars have a built-in facility to retract the rear brake calliper pistons with either a spanner, screwdriver or Allen key via the rear of the calliper. Check whether this technique applies to your car by consulting the car's handbook or via a web search. **Caution!** If your car features built-in piston retractors, **do not** use a reset tool or force to retract the pistons prior to installing new pads.

• Next set up the calliper as if you were

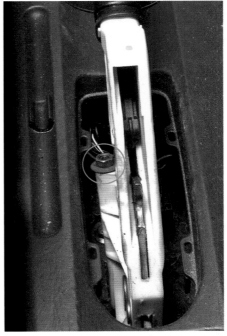

Fig 67. Typical parking brake cable adjuster at lever end.

Fig 66. Typical brake calliper piston reset tool.

Fig 68. Transparent container with a small amount of brake fluid covering end of the tube. Better still, is a tube with a one-way valve.

Fig 69. Calliper piston reset tool in use.

parking brake cable so that it's the brake is fully applied after four clicks (heard as you pull the brake lever).
• Pump the brake pedal to bring the brake pads to their correct position.
• Top up the brake fluid to 'Max' and replace the reservoir cap.
• Brake bleeding is recommended (see chapter 3) to ensure the brake is purged of air. **Caution!** Bleeding is essential if there is any change to brake pedal 'feel' (ie: sponginess) or it travels further.
• Take the car for a test drive. The handbrake may need further adjustment as the pads settle into position.

going to bleed it (Fig 68), and then open the bleed nipple as the piston is retracted, so that displaced fluid collects in a jar without allowing air to enter the system. It is essential that the tube between the nipple and jar remains immersed in the fluid in the jar while the bleed nipple is open.
• If applicable, insert the piston reset tool between the calliper and the piston and wind the tool in to take up the slack (Fig 69).
• If you're using a calliper piston reset tool, turn it slowly clockwise or anti-clockwise, as required, to 'screw' the piston back until it's flush with the housing. If your car has a built-in calliper retraction device, use this instead.
Caution! Close the bleed nipple when the piston is fully retracted.

Installing new brake pads
• Follow the same procedure as for the front brake pads (see page 33), but, when it comes to repositioning the outer part of the calliper over the rear pads, fit the uppermost bolt first, pivot the outer calliper down over the pads, and then fit the lower bolt. This may take a bit of effort because of the retaining springs on the top of the pad (if fitted).
• You will also need to re-adjust the

Replacing a brake disc

Fig 70. Ventilated brake disc top, unventilated bottom.

Caution! When fitting a new brake disc always renew the other disc on the same axle, too.

It's possible to change the brake discs without removing the brake pads, but for ease it's recommended that the pads are removed to stop them falling out when the outer calliper is released/pivoted up.

Don't contaminate the new disc braking surface with grease or dirt from your hands. Note that the new discs may have a protective coating which will need to be removed with a solvent.

Required
Jack/s

Axle stands (jack stands)
New discs
Spanners
Half inch drive socket set
Torque wrench
G-clamp (front only)
Piston spreader (front only)
Piston reset tool (rear only), if applicable

FRONT

Removing the calliper

Note: Some cars (eg: Ford and BMW)
use 7mm hex head bolts to retain
the outer part of the calliper. This is a
non-standard size, so you will need to
purchase the appropriate socket.

• With the brake pads removed and
the outer part of the calliper pivoted
upward, you have good access to the
two large bolts that secure the whole

Fig 71. Typical calliper mounting bolts.

calliper assembly to the steering/
suspension arm (Fig 71).
• Undo the two bolts, remove the
calliper, and support it by hanging it from
a piece of wire or resting it on a small
box – it's not a good idea to leave the
calliper hanging from the brake hose!

Removing the old disc

• Remove the screw/s that secure
the brake disc to the hub (Fig 72), if
fitted. These screws are normally only
finger-tight (enough to hold the disc in
position). When the wheel is refitted the
wheel nuts/bolts provide extra tightness,
and clamp the disc between the wheel
and the hub.

Fig 72. Typical brake disc securing screw.

• You should now be able to pull the
brake disc off the hub. If the disc is
difficult to remove it's probably due to
a small amount of corrosion between it
and the hub. Simply tap the brake disc
from behind with a soft-faced hammer
or piece of wood.
• With the disc removed, clean the
shoulder it sits on (to remove corrosion
and dirt) with a piece of 800 grade wet-
and-dry abrasive paper or a wire brush.
Then apply a very thin coat of copper
grease to the shoulder.

Fitting the new disc

• Position the new brake disc in place of

37

the old one, ensuring that the back of the disc and the face of the hub are clean; dirt trapped between these surfaces could cause the disc to run out of true.
• Replace the disc securing screw/s, if applicable.

Refitting the calliper
• Refit the calliper assembly to the steering/suspension arm by installing the two large bolts. **Caution!** These bolts need to be secure, so it's recommended you apply thread locking fluid (such as Loctite) to their threads, and tighten them as much as you can by hand using a half inch drive socket and the standard T-bar from the socket set. You should be able to find the correct torque setting by doing a web search.

Refitting the brake pads
• Push the brake piston back into the calliper assembly (page 35), so that the pads will fit around the thicker new disc.
• Slot the pads back into position.
• Pivot the outer calliper back down, and refit the securing bolt.
• Double-check everything, and pump the footbrake a few times to bring the new pads into contact with the disc.
• Refit the road wheel and lower the car to the ground using the jack.
• Retighten the wheel nuts/bolts and take the car for a short drive.

   Caution! Initially, the brakes will be less responsive. Allow 100-200 miles for them to bed in and become fully effective.

REAR

Removing the brake pads & calliper
Follow previous instructions on how to remove the rear brake pads and calliper.

Removing the old disc
• Follow the same procedure as for removing the front disc (previous page), undoing the disc securing screws; if present.

Fitting the new disc & refitting the brake pads
• Fit the new disc on the hub and tighten the disc securing screws (if applicable).
• Refit the calliper assembly to the suspension upright/strut by installing and tightening the two large bolts. **Caution!** These bolts need to be secure, so it's recommended that you apply thread locking fluid (such as Loctite) to their threads and tighten them as much as you can by hand using a half inch drive socket and the standard T-bar from the socket set. You should be able to find the correct torque setting by doing a web search.
• Refit the pads as per Preparing to install new brake pads and Installing new brake pads on pages 35 and 36.

• Check that everything is where it should be before refitting the road wheel/s and lowering the car to the ground using the jack.

Bleeding the brake system
• You may now need to bleed the brake system (as detailed in chapter 3) because brake fluid was released via the bleed valve when resetting the calliper piston.
• With the system bled, check the level of brake fluid in the reservoir, and tighten the cap.
• Pump the footbrake with the engine running to take up any slack in the brakes.
• Apply the parking brake a number of times to allow the auto adjusters to do their job.

Rear brake drum removal & brake shoe replacement

There are two methods of removing rear drums, depending on the make of car, so information specific to each is marked throughout this section, as either 'A' or 'B.'

Fig 73. Drum with securing screws (arrowed) identifying it as 'type A.'

If after removing the wheel you can see a cross-head or star screw set into the drum (Fig 73), the drum can be removed by releasing the screw/s (without needing to split the rear bearing), and you should refer to 'A.'

Fig 74. Drum without securing screws identifying it as 'type B.'

If no securing screws are visible (Fig 74), you'll need to split the bearing in order to remove the drum, and you should refer to 'B.'

• Jack up and safely support the rear of the car, release the parking brake and remove the rear wheel/s to determine which method to follow.

Caution! The brake shoes for both rear wheels must be renewed at the same time.

Removing the drum

It may be possible to fully release the brake shoes (moving them away from the drum) so that the drum will pull off easily:

• Check the rear of the backplate for a small vertical slot below where the brake hose enters the plate. If there is an access slot you will see a small toothed wheel inside the brake assembly. Using a small, flat-bladed screwdriver, rotate the wheel downward to release the brake shoes.

Type A

• Remove the brake drum securing screw/s.

• Tap the brake drum outward around the back edge with a soft-faced hammer to release it from the stub axle. **Caution:** Do not hit the brake drum with an ordinary hammer as this will crack it, rendering it useless; also take care not to damage the brake backplate.

The brake shoes are the only items resisting drum removal, so, with the drum under tension, tapping it will shock the shoes and cause them to move toward the backplate to which they are attached. It may take some time to remove the drum, but it's better to be careful than to damage the backplate.

With the drum removed you now have access to the brake shoes.

Type B

• Lever out the centre domed cover

using a small, flat-bladed screwdriver to access the stub axle nut and bearing. This nut may be locked by a multi-nut (Fig 51), a staked nut (Fig 52), or a cage and spring pin (Fig 75). If applicable, release the stake completely with a flat-bladed screwdriver, or pull out the spring pin and remove the cage to release the nut. Undo the stub axle nut.

Note: If this nut is excessively tight, and you find the drum is turning, refit the wheel and lower the car to the ground so you can more easily apply greater force with the socket wrench.

• With the nut loose, raise the car and remove the wheel, and make sure the handbrake is released.

• Remove the stub axle nut and place it on either a clean piece of cloth or card so you do not contaminate the grease on its inner side.

• Remove the brake drum and place it rim side down to stop the outer roller bearing falling out.

You now have access to the brake shoes.

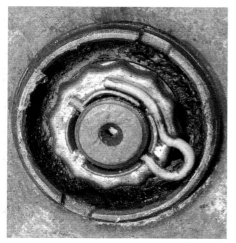

Fig 75. Nut cage and spring pin locking device.

Inspecting the drum

• Check the drum for cracks, and for excessive wear inside, where the shoes bear against the drum walls. The amount of wear can be determined by examining the depth of the ridges on the outer edges of where the shoes have been in contact (Fig 76). If the ridge is more than a couple of millimetres ($\frac{1}{16}$in) deep, it's advisable to renew the drums. **Caution!** both old drums on the same axle should be replaced by new items at the same time. New drums will require time to bed in (around 200 miles).

Fig 76. Discernable wear ridges within the brake drum.

Rear drum brake types

There are two common types of rear drum brake assembly (as shown in Figs 77 & 78/79). The most important difference is the design of the brake auto adjuster, which is covered in more detail later, but you should also be aware that, depending on the type of brake assembly, retraction springs are fitted either behind or on top of the brake shoes; also the shoe retaining devices are different, although both pin-based.

Opposite:
Top; Fig 77. Rear drum brake components: 'type 1' for the purposes of this book.
Fig 78. Rear drum brake components: 'type 2' for the purposes of this book.

Pistons

Backplate

Brake cylinder

Spreader bar

Long spring

Small spring

Auto adjuster

Adjuster lock arm

Shoe retaining clip

Shoe retaining clip

Handbrake arm

Brake shoe

Brake shoe

Handbrake cable

Friction material

Retaining spring

Bottom pivot

Pistons

Backplate

Brake cylinder

Auto adjuster toothed wheel

Shoe retaining spring & cap

Auto adjuster arm

Handbrake arm

Brake shoe

Shoe retaining spring & cap

Brake shoe

Retaining spring

Handbrake cable

Bottom pivot

Friction material

Fig 79. An alternative version of a 'type 2' design is different in detail, but overall follows the same design principles.

Brake auto adjusters

Now that the drum has been removed it's possible to identify which type of auto adjuster is fitted. As the brake shoes wear, these auto adjusters maintain a minimum distance between the brake shoes and the brake drum; moving the brake shoes outwards towards the surface of the brake drum as the friction material wears. You will need to release the brake auto adjusters in order to remove the old brake shoes and make room for the new, thicker ones.

Fig 80. Auto adjuster with lower toothed sprung arm attached to the brake shoe.

• In Fig 80, the auto adjuster is attached to the actual shoe, and is released by pushing the lower toothed sprung arm (arrowed in Fig 80) downward.
• The other type of auto adjuster is a toothed wheel, as shown in Fig 81. Rotate the top of the toothed wheel toward the backplate whilst holding the ratchet arm away from the wheel (so that the adjuster withdraws into the tube) with the tip of a screwdriver.
Note: This type of auto adjuster acts as the spreader bar; pushing the brake shoes apart to help ensure they stay in the correct position when in use.
• Identify which type of rear drum

Fig 81. Typical toothed wheel auto adjuster.

Fig 82. Shoe retaining clip type 1.

assembly is fitted to your car, and familiarise yourself with all the components and how they are fitted and whether the features of your car's brake assembly are identical and, if not, make a note of what differs.

Fig 83. Shoe retaining clip type 2.

Removing old brake shoes

Now is a good time to photograph the brake assembly on your car for reference, especially if it differs from the typical examples shown here.

Note: The basic procedure for changing brake shoes is the same, regardless of the type of auto adjuster present.

• Fully release the auto adjuster, as explained above (depending on the type fitted).
• Release the brake shoe retaining clips of the type shown in Fig 82 by pushing down the open end of the U-spring to release the pin head from its seat and then pulling the spring off.

There's another type of retainer as shown in Fig 83 that requires you to push a cup against a coil spring, then to twist the cup through 90 degrees to release it from the retaining pin.

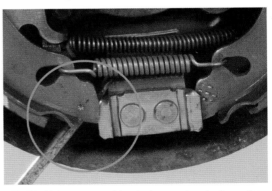

Fig 84. Using a screwdriver to lever out and release the shoe end from the bottom pivot.

• Using a screwdriver, ease one of the brake shoes out of the lower pivot assembly, as shown in Fig 84.

Note: You must do this at the pivot end of the shoes (the opposite end to the brake cylinder). If you try to do this at the brake cylinder end of the shoes you will damage the rubber seals.
• Now do the same with the other brake

43

shoe, so that both shoes are released. This allows you to remove the lower spring.

• Check that the auto adjuster is fully released to allow maximum movement between the shoe heads.

• Holding the bottom of the shoes together (allowing the tops to move further apart as they pivot on the spreader bar/auto adjuster bar), gently pull the shoes downward, making sure you are not trapping the piston seals, and remove.

• Push both the pistons into the brake cylinder so that the piston ends protrude equally. **Note:** Make sure you push both pistons in at the same time to centralise them, and avoid one popping out, which will necessitate bleeding the brake system.

Dismantling the brake assembly

Note: If the brake assembly on your car has a tube/toothed wheel auto adjuster, the long spring must be refitted with the coiled end opposite the ratchet end of the adjuster.

If the auto adjuster is on the actual brake shoe (similar to that shown in Fig 80), the springs are usually fitted outside of the brake shoes, and may not be coloured.

• Remove the long spring from the top of the shoes (just below the spreader bar and brake adjuster). The spring is easily released using a pair of pliers. **Note:** You are working at the end with the actual coil spring, not the extended end.

A screwdriver pushed between the handbrake arm and the shoe it's attached to, will allow the handbrake arm to be extended and the handbrake cable to be disconnected, if necessary.

• Using a pair of pliers, disconnect the small handbrake spring.

• You can now remove the spreader arm/auto adjuster bar, so that the brake

Fig 85. Rotating the brake shoe outward to disconnect the handbrake cable from the handbrake arm.

assembly is fully dismantled (Figs 86 & 87).

Fitting new brake shoes

Note: The 'trailing' brake shoe is the shoe closest to the rear of the car.

Refitting the shoes is essentially the reversal of removal. It's possible that the handbrake arm on the new set of shoes may be on the opposite side of the trailing brake shoe than it was on the shoes you removed.

To ensure correct fitting of the adjuster or spreader arm, follow the instructions below.

Type 1 brakes

Refitting the spreader bar (all references are to Fig 86).

• See double slot 'A' + 'B' on spreader bar. Slot 'A' on the trailing shoe fits in slot 'A' on the spreader bar.

• The handbrake arm fits into slot 'B.'

• The auto adjuster is threaded on to the spreader arm so the auto adjuster sits in position 'C.'

• The shoe fits in position 'D.'

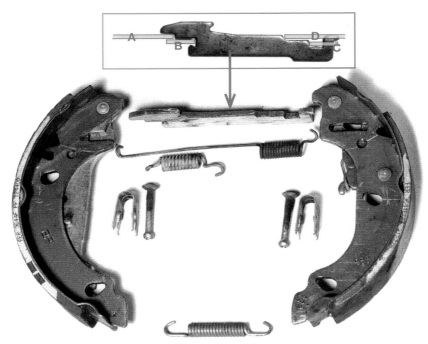

Fig 86. Components of brake assembly (type 1). Inset shows spreader bar (may look different) viewed side on and how it engages with various components (see text).

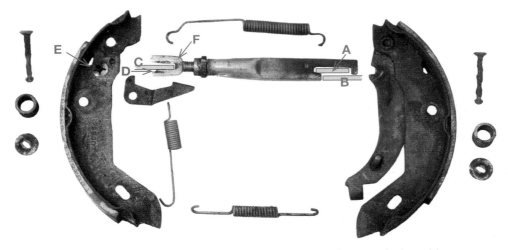

Fig 87. Components of brake assembly (type 2). Note that the auto adjuster arm is shown lying on its side: in situ it would be turned 90 degrees so that the slot at left hand end is facing outward from the brake backplate. For key to how auto adjuster arm engages with various components, see text.

45

• The spreader bar may have to be turned over to be fitted correctly, depending on the position of the handbrake arm.

Type 2 brakes

Refitting the auto adjuster arm (all references are to Fig 87).

• See slot 'A' and capture slot 'B' on auto adjuster arm. The handbrake arm rests in slot 'A' and the trailing shoe fits in position 'B.'

• The leading shoe fits into slot 'C' so that the slot is just above the ratchet arm pivot 'E.' Ensure that cutout 'D' is on the outside as this allows the ratchet arm to move freely.

Type 1 & 2 brakes

• Before reassembly, ensure the brake shoe auto adjuster is fully returned to its starting position. This can be done with just finger pressure by pulling down the lock arm and pushing the auto adjuster bar back or screwing the adjuster end ('F' in Fig 87) of the auto adjuster into the tube.

• Wash your hands thoroughly to prevent contaminating the new brake shoes, then apply a thin smear of copper grease to the raised portions of the backplate (marked in white in Fig 88) to aid brake shoe movement.

• Refit the handbrake cable: using a screwdriver to hold the handbrake arm forward, offer the shoe up to the cable. With the end of the cable through its entry hole, hold the nipple on the end of the cable with a pair of vice grip pliers. You can now push the shoe against the cable outer to compress the spring whilst holding the end with the grips. This will let the cable fully enter the arm and allow you to guide it to its correct position. Other types of shoe have a straightforward cable entry.

Fig 88. The white markings have been added to this picture to show the raised areas of the backplate to which you should apply a light smear of copper grease.

Type 1 brakes

• Fit the small spring first (some assemblies do not have this spring) by attaching it to the shoe and then the arm (Fig 89). Twist the arm up into its proper position (Fig 90).

• You can now fit the long spring (behind the small spring, if a small spring is fitted). Ease the small spring away from the shoe with a screwdriver and thread the long spring into its correct position (refer to Fig 77).

Fig 89. Fitting the small spring.

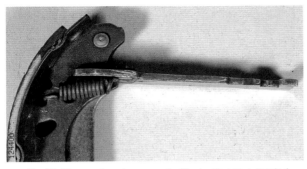

Fig 90. The small spring correctly fitted with arm extended.

Type 1 & 2 brakes

• Attach the spreader bar or auto adjuster arm between the two shoes and connect the long spring between the shoes. Note: Ensure the spreader/adjuster bar is fitted correctly on to the shoes.

• Mount the tops of the brake shoes correctly against the centre of the piston

Fig 91. Close-up of a wheel cylinder piston (not all have these slots to engage the shoes).

Fig 92. Bottom pivot with shoe ends correctly fitted.

ends (in the piston slots, if they have slots) (Fig 91).

• Fit the bottom of the shoes to the pivot plate, as shown in Fig 92.

• Refit the bottom spring to hold the brake shoes in position.

• Check everything is correct, and that you have not damaged the rubber piston seals.

• Check that the brake auto-adjuster is fully returned (almost totally behind the shoe or fully returned inside the tube, depending on the type fitted), as this will make it easier to fit the drum.

• Refit the shoes' securing pins and their springs and locking caps or their clips. The pins are pushed in from the rear of the backplate and are secured by the clips or springs and locking caps. The coil springs require a lot of pressure to compress them with the locking cap in a pair of pliers, so you may need the help of an assistant to hold the pin in position. Lock the pin spring in position by turning the locking cap 90 degrees on the end of the pin.

Refitting the brake drum
Type A & B drums

• You may have to wiggle the drum to get it over the shoes and seated on the hub. If you find that the drum will not go on, remove it completely and alter the position of the shoes. The shoes can be slid up or down a little, and also to the left or right, to centre them.

• If you do reposition the shoes check the auto-adjusters again, as they can easily be disturbed when moving the shoes.

Type A drum

• With the drum in position, tighten the securing screw/s but note that these should not be over-tight.

Type B drum

• When refitting the drum it's possible to push the outer part of the roller bearing out, so place a cloth or a piece of clean cardboard underneath to stop it from becoming contaminated with dirt if this does happen. If the outer part of the roller bearing does get contaminated, it will need to be thoroughly cleaned with a proprietary solvent, allowed to dry, and then be re-greased. If re-greasing, use the correct type of bearing grease and ensure all the roller surfaces are covered with a thin coating before refitting.

• With the drum in position, refit and tighten the bearing nut to the correct setting using a torque wrench. Over tightness or looseness will cause excessive wear on the bearing and lead to its failure. A web search will usually find the correct torque setting for your car. **Caution!** If the nut was locked by a cage and spring pin both the cage and spring pin must be refitted. If it was locked by a stake, use a punch to punch a section of the nut's staking collar into the groove in the axle shaft.

• Refit the domed cover and tap it gently in the middle to set it. Note: It's a tension fit, so there is no need to hammer it in! If the cover appears loose after fitting, a sharp tap in the centre of the dome will tighten it.

Type A & B drums

• If you do have access to a brake shoe adjuster through the rear of the backplate, adjust it until the drum just starts to bind on the brake shoes. Once it binds, release the adjuster, a click at a time, until the drum just runs free. There may be a slight sound of rubbing, but this could just be the new shoes bearing against the wear ridge inside the drum.

• Refit the wheel, tighten its securing nut or bolts and spin it around. Apply the handbrake, several times with the wheel spinning to adjust the shoes and to confirm that it stops the wheel. If there is no external access to the auto adjusters, be aware that handbrake function may be slightly impaired until the handbrake has been applied sufficiently often to bring the shoes into proper adjustment.

• If all appears to be working correctly, proceed to lower the car using the jack.

Final checks

• Fully tighten the wheel nuts/bolts, and replace the wheel trim, if fitted.

• Start the engine and pump the brake pedal. Also apply the handbrake at least ten times to take up any slack that may have been created whilst working on the system, and to allow the shoes to attain their correct position against the drum.

• Take the car for a test drive to allow the 'shine' to be scrubbed off the new shoes. Remember, you have been working on the braking system, and the shoes need to bed into the drum, over a few miles of use, so take care.

Note: If you have changed drums and shoes together, it will take longer for the brakes to bed in.

three

Bleeding the brake hydraulic system

It's sometimes necessary to bleed (remove air from) the brake system after fitting new brake pads.

We do not recommend that you bleed brake systems by pumping the brake pedal and constantly topping-up the master cylinder fluid reservoir. There are three reasons for this advice:

1) The pumping method allows the piston in the master cylinder to travel beyond its normal range (which can damage the piston seal).

2) There is a danger of introducing air into the hydraulic system if the fluid level in the reservoir runs too low.

3) Two people are needed: one to pump the pedal, the other to open bleed valves.

There are a number of products available on the high street which allow efficient, safe, and single-handed brake system bleeding, all of which work in a similar manner. For demonstration purposes, the Gunson Eezibleed kit

Fig 93. Automatic, one-person brake bleeding kit.

is used in the following text/photo sequence. **Caution!** the procedure described here is general, and whichever kit you choose will come with

49

its own specific set of instructions that you must follow for safety's sake.

All modern vehicles have fail-safe split braking systems with what are called 'tandem' master cylinders (two pistons acting on two separate circuits, so that if one circuit fails the other will still operate on two wheels). Some tandem master cylinder designs require that the bled valves at two wheels (usually diagonally opposite) are open simultaneously during the bleeding operation. Consult your handbook, or internet sources for information on your particular car.

The Gunson kit (Fig 93) consists of:
1x Bottle to hold the new brake fluid
1x Bottle cap assembly complete with tyre connector
3x Plastic pipes (different sizes) to drain old fluid from bleed valve into a suitable container
4x Plastic caps to fit different types of brake fluid reservoir

Required
Cloth (brake fluid can damage the vehicle paintwork)
Correct brake fluid (check handbook)
The correct size ring spanner for the bleed valve
A suitable length of transparent flexible tube, which will fit tightly on the bleed valve nipple
A container to safely collect expelled brake fluid

Note: The road wheel has been removed to allow greater visibility: you don't have to do this, but it will give you easier access.

• Remove the dust cap from the relevant bleed valve nipple (if present) and fit the ring spanner on the nipple in such a position that it will allow the nipple to be opened.

Fig 94. Transparent container with a small amount of brake fluid in which the end of the bleed tube is immersed.

• Attach the bleed tube to the nipple with its open end in the container that will be used to safely catch expelled fluid (Fig 94).
• Attach the fluid feed pipe to the correct size reservoir cap, as per the kit's instructions, and fit onto the reservoir (do not over tighten).
• Attach the fluid bottle (empty).
• Check that the pressure in the spare wheel is as per the kit's instructions.
• Attach the air pipe to the spare wheel to pressurise the system, and check for any leaks – tighten if/where, necessary.

If all is okay, remove the air pipe from the spare wheel, then, if required by the kit's instructions, lower the pressure in the spare wheel by pushing in the pinion in the inflation valve until the required pressure is reached.

• Remove the fluid bottle and fill it to

at least the lower fluid mark with new brake fluid (do not reattach yet).

• With the top off the reservoir, open the bleed valve to allow some brake fluid to drain through using gravity until the reservoir is about half full, then close the bleed valve.

• Reattach the fluid bottle containing the fresh fluid to the brake reservoir feed.

• Pressurise the system by attaching the air pipe to the spare wheel valve.

• Undo the bleed valve on the calliper or wheel cylinder (about half a turn to ensure there is no restriction) to allow the old brake fluid to be pushed out and into the container (Fig 95).

• As soon as the expelled fluid running through the tube shows no air bubbles, close the bleed valve.

• Depressurise the bleed system by removing the air pipe attached to the spare wheel, before removing the reservoir feed cap.

• Remove the drain pipe from calliper or wheel cylinder and refit the valve dust cap (if present).

• Remove the fluid feed cap from reservoir and refit the original cap (top up with brake fluid, if necessary).

• Take the car for a short test drive.

Caution! If the brake pedal feels 'spongy,' it's likely that there's still air in the brake hydraulic system, meaning you will need to bleed it again.

• Don't forget to re-inflate the spare wheel to its normal pressure.

If you need to bleed the whole brake hydraulic system (necessary to change the brake fluid) then you should contact your vehicle manufacturer, as there may be a particular sequence in which the brakes should be bled. Once the sequence is known, go around the car bleeding each individual brake (maybe a pair of brakes – see advice at the beginning of this chapter) in the correct order. After bleeding the brake at each

Fig 95. Full bleeding kit in place and connected to spare wheel. The bleed valve can now be opened to bleed the hydraulic system.

wheel, check that you still have fluid above the minimum mark in the feed bottle. **Caution!** On no account allow the brake fluid to fall below the minimum mark as this may allow air to enter the brake system!

Most manufacturers recommend that the brake system is fully bled at least every two years (consult the car's handbook).

Caution! Do not re-use old brake fluid. Do not mix different brake fluids.

Important! Dispose of used brake fluid at approved disposal sites.

four
Engine oil & oil filter change

Fig 96. Typical types of oil filter (colours vary).

It's important to first make sure that you have the correct type of engine oil and filter for your car (check the car's handbook for details). If you've already purchased the filter, visually check that

it matches the one already fitted – errors are easily made, and you wouldn't want to find it was the wrong type after removing the old filter.

Required
Spanner, hex driver or square drive (depending on the type of drain plug)
Oil filter (if being changed)
Engine oil (as specified in the car's handbook)
Funnel (if required)
Container to drain the old oil into (capable of holding at least five litres)
Canister-type oil filter removal tool (recommended)

Draining the engine oil
• Warm the engine from cold by letting it run for three to four minutes and then switching it off. The engine oil will then be warm enough to flow well.

Fig 97. Typical oil filler cap with yellow oil can symbol.

Caution! Make sure you do not let the engine get so hot that you risk burning yourself when the oil is released.

• With the bonnet open, remove the oil filler cap (Fig 97). This will normally have 'OIL' written on it, or the symbol of an oil can in yellow.

• If your car has a belly pan fitted (ie: a cover fitted beneath the entire engine bay), it may have a hatch to access the drain plug, or you may need to remove the belly pan completely to gain access to the drain plug. Again, this is dependant on the make and model of car. If fitted, the belly pan will normally be held by plastic screws. You may find that some of these screws have been replaced by cable ties (where they have broken in the past).

• The drain plug will be set into the bottom of the sump/oil pan, or on the side close to the bottom (Fig 98).

The sump is where all the oil that

Oil filter (canister-type)

Sump/oil pan

Drain plug

Fig 98. The underside of a typical car showing the drain plug located on the sump/oil pan at the lowest part of the engine, and the oil filter.

Fig 99. Typical sump drain plug (square drive-type).

Fig 99a. Typical sump drain plug (bolt-type).

you put into the engine is stored. It typically holds four to six litres of oil, depending on the engine size (check the car's handbook on this important point).
• Clean the drain plug and its surrounding area with a stiff brush.
• Place the empty container under the drain plug in the sump to catch the used oil.
• Undo and remove the drain plug

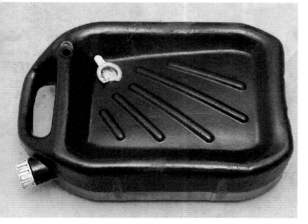

Fig 100. Typical oil catcher/container.

(Fig 99 and 99a) to allow the oil to drain out. Be careful not to round the corners off the plug when undoing it, particularly if it's a hex or square drive fitting.
Note: You can jack up the car to make it easier to loosen the plug (taking the usual precautions regarding safety) if need be, but the car needs to be lowered for the oil to drain completely.
• Allow the oil to drain into the container for as long as possible. When it's finished draining from the sump wipe clean the drain plug and the area around the drain hole with a clean rag.
• Replace the drain plug and tighten it. **Caution!** The sump may be made of an alloy, so do not over-tighten the plug or you could strip the thread.

If you are renewing the oil filter, then continue reading, if not, go straight to 'Adding new engine oil.'

Removing the oil filter (canister type)
Assess how you are going to remove the oil filter. It could be

Fig 101. Typical canister-type oil filter low down at the rear of an engine.

Fig 102. Typical canister-type oil filter low down at the front of an engine.

located in a number of places on the engine (Figs 101-103 show a variety of locations), and be accessible from either above or below the car. It's worth while considering how to go about this, because once you start there's no going back!

- If necessary clean the oil filter body to give a good grip.
- Move the used oil container to a position directly beneath the oil filter.
- It's normal for the filter to be only finger-tight when fitted, so try and remove it by turning it anti-clockwise by hand.

Note: Oil will be released from the filter during removal.

If you have successfully removed the oil filter by hand, proceed to 'Fitting the new oil filter,' if not, continue reading.

Using a tool to remove the oil filter

If you are unable to undo the oil filter by hand, there are various tools available to help, and the one you use may be determined by the amount of access you have to the oil filter. Some of these tools are shown in Figs 104 to 109 and the method for using each is described:

Caution! Unusual, but do be aware that it's possible that the filter will begin to collapse when pressure is applied using the following tools and

Fig 103. Typical canister-type oil filter at the front of the engine, but visible from above.

methods. If this happens you must stop immediately. If you cannot unscrew the filter using reasonable force, and without distorting it, you need to get a garage to change the filter for you. DO NOT drive the car if oil has begun to leak from the oil filter body or its joint with the engine.

Chain/fabric strap

Fig 106. Chain tool fitted (same method for the canvas tool).

Fig 104. Oil filter removal chain strap tool.

Fig 107. Chain tool fitted with socket (same method for the canvas tool).

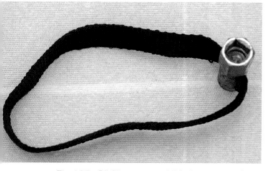

Fig 105. Oil filter removal fabric strap tool.

• Fit the tool over the filter as close to the engine as possible (Fig 106).
• Turn anti-clockwise so that the tool rolls in on itself.
• Holding the tool in position, attach a socket or ring spanner to it (Fig 107).

• Using the socket/spanner, continue to turn anti-clockwise; the tool will grip on itself and to the filter. Take care that the tool or socket/spanner are not fouling the engine block or other items close to the filter area when turning.
• The filter should begin to turn anti-clockwise and, as soon as it does, it's usually possible to unscrew it the

56

rest of the way by hand until it's free of the engine.

Filter pliers
• Fit the tool over the squared-off edges at the very end of the filter and turn anti-clockwise. **Note:** The squared-off sections of the filter body, designed for this type of tool to grip, do not extend for the full depth of the filter body.

Fig 108. Oil filter removal pliers.

Fig 109. Filter pliers in use.

Fitting the new oil filter (canister type)
• With the old filter removed, wipe around the engine filter mounting with a clean cloth to clean away any dirt, taking care not to introduce dirt into the area which the filter covers.
• Rub a small amount of oil over the rubber seal (Fig 110) of the new filter using your finger. This will aid sealing and also prevent the oil filter seal bunching, or baking onto the engine once fitted, making the filter difficult to remove.

Fig 110. Canister-type filter rubber seal.

• Being very careful not to contaminate the filter face or seal by brushing against dirty areas, offer-up the new filter to the mounting and then screw it on in a clockwise direction.
• Tighten as much as possible using only hand pressure.

Removing & replacing the oil filter element (separate element type)
If your vehicle uses an oil filter with a separate, removable, element the filter unit may not be directly fitted to the

engine, but remote from it. Whether directly attached to the engine or remote, the filter will still take on the general appearance of the canister-type filters shown in this chapter, but if remote will have two pipes leading to the filter holder unit. Take a good look at this unit as it may well have a oil drain plug fitted, this would allow you to drain the filter unit before removal.

• If a drain plug is fitted, drain the oil from the unit and then replace the drain plug. The filter element holder body is secured to its base by a central long bolt, which you should now remove. Remember there will be oil spillage

when removing the filter holder and element unless you were able to drain it as previously described.

• Dispose of the old filter element but keep hold of the rubber seal if it's in good condition (there may be no new seal with the new element). There will be a seal of some type at the bolt head end of the holder body.

• Wipe around the end of the element holder, and its mounting, with a clean cloth. Apply a small amount of oil to the rubber seal/s and fit them in position.

• Insert the new element into the element holder and refit the element holder to its mounting.

• In order not to apply too much

Oil filler cap (removed)

Cam or rocker box cover

Engine oil level dipstick

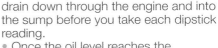

pressure when tightening the element holder retaining bolt, use a spanner to tighten it and the pressure of just one finger: this will stop you over-tightening the filter bolt and distorting the seals.

Adding new engine oil

• Check that both the filter and drain plug are securely fitted.

• Pour the new oil into the engine slowly (using a funnel if necessary), allowing time for it to drain through the engine (Fig 111).

• After pouring in about two litres/four pints, start checking the amount of oil in the engine via the dipstick – you'll need to wait a minute or two for the oil to

drain down through the engine and into the sump before you take each dipstick reading.

• Once the oil level reaches the 'maximum' mark on the dipstick, stop adding oil.

• Start the engine and allow it to run for a minute as this will fill the oil filter with oil.

• Stop the engine, then, after allowing ten minutes or so for oil to drain back into the sump, check the oil level and top up as required.

• Once the dipstick oil level reads 'maximum,' do not add any more oil – too much oil can do as much damage to the engine as too little.

• Replace the oil filler cap securely, and close the bonnet.

• Take the car for a short drive, then check for oil leaks around both the filter and sump plug. Check the engine oil level again once the engine has cooled. Top up to maximum level, if required.

Fig 111. Refilling the engine with the correct grade of oil.

Fig 112. Removing the dipstick.

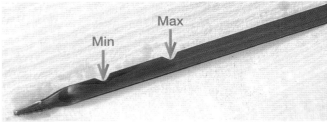

Fig 113. Checking the oil level on the dipstick.

Max
Min

five

Sparkplugs

Removal, inspection, maintenance & fitting

Note: This chapter does not apply if your car has a diesel engine.

Required
Correct size sparkplug socket
Clean cloth
Wire brush
Feeler gauge or 'all-in-one sparkplug tool'
Very fine wet-and-dry paper
New sparkplugs, if required

Fig 114. Different designs of sparkplug.

Fig 115. The external anatomy of a typical sparkplug (courtesy Nippon Denso).

Sealing washer

Centre electrode

Insulation recess

Insulator

Plug lead connector nipple (not used in some applications, in which case it can be unscrewed and removed)

Insulation nose

Earth/Ground electrode

Removal

- When the engine is cold, open and secure the bonnet (hood), then locate the sparkplug high tension (HT) leads (wires) connector caps (Figs 116/117).
- Pull the first sparkplug connector off the top of the sparkplug; do not pull the lead itself, grip the connector cap instead (Fig 118).

Note: Do not remove all the leads at the same time – it's important that they all go back onto the same sparkplugs, in the correct order, for the engine to run properly.

- With the lead disconnected,

you'll see the plug top. If the sparkplug is shallow-mounted and quite visible (Fig 119), use a small paintbrush to remove dirt from around the plug, so that it won't fall into the engine once the plug is removed.

Fig 116. Sparkplug leads and connector caps on the side of an engine.

Fig 117. Sparkplug leads (wires) and connector caps on top of an engine.

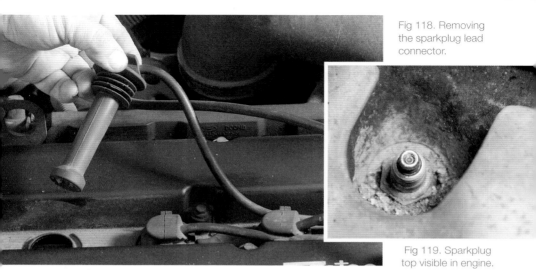

Fig 118. Removing the sparkplug lead connector.

Fig 119. Sparkplug top visible in engine.

• Fit the sparkplug socket (Fig 120) onto the plug. **Note:** Sparkplug sockets have a rubber grommet inside to grip the plug and aid removal if the plug hole is in a deep recess, it also protects the fragile insulator. Push down slightly on the socket so that the top of the plug goes into the grommet.

• Turn the socket anti-clockwise to undo the plug. It should be tight, but you shouldn't have to exert excessive force to get it moving. If the plug doesn't move, try spraying it with penetrating oil and leaving it for a few minutes so that the oil seeps into the thread. If you still can't remove the plug after this, you should take the car to a garage. **Caution!** Do not force the plug – the thread in the cylinder head could get damaged or, worse still, the plug head could snap off as a result.

If the sparkplug moves, but then begins to bind, apply some penetrating oil or a drop of engine oil around it. Then slowly work the plug back and forth to free it – remember, you could cause damage by being too forceful.

• Once the plug is moving, continue undoing it slowly, until it's fully removed.

Inspection
Remove the sparkplug from its socket and compare the plug electrodes with those in the following pictures to understand how well the engine is running, and what action to take, if any.

Normal
The colour of the insulator nose is between whitish or yellowish-grey and russet. The engine is running normally: correct plugs, correct fuelling

Fig 120. Different size sparkplug sockets. Note the protective rubber grommets (arrowed).

Fig Plug 01.
Normal.

Fig Plug 04.
Soot fouling.

Fig Plug 02.
Normal.

the wrong air and fuel mixture. Other reasons could be an extremely dirty air filter or that the car is used for extremely short distances only.

Effect
Misfiring. Poor cold starts.

Solution
Check and clean the air filter. Have the fuel-injection system (or carburettor) checked by a garage.

and timing okay, no misfiring and no overheating.

Oil fouling
The insulator nose, electrodes, and sparkplug shell is covered by a shiny, oily layer of soot or carbon.

Soot fouling
The insulator nose, electrodes, and sparkplug shell is covered with a felt-textured, matt black coating of soot.

Cause
Fuel-injection (carburettor on older cars) could be out of adjustment, causing

Fig Plug 05.
Oil fouling.

Fig Plug 03.
Soot fouling.

Cause
Severe wear of piston rings, cylinder walls or valve seals/guides.

Effect
Misfiring. Starting difficulties.

Fig Plug 06.
Oil fouling.

Solution
Replace the sparkplugs. If there's no improvement after this an engine overhaul is required (beyond the scope of this book).

Eroded centre electrode
Cause
Failure to observe sparkplug replacement intervals (see car's handbook).

Fig Plug 07.
Eroded centre electrode.

Effect
Misfiring, especially during acceleration (because the ignition voltage is not adequate for bridging the wider electrode gap). Starting difficulties.

Solution
New sparkplugs.

Fitting a sparkplug
If after inspection the sparkplug is normal (ie: it doesn't have to be replaced), continue reading. If you are fitting a new sparkplug, skip 'Cleaning' and go to 'Setting the plug gap.'

Cleaning
• Clean the plug insulator by wiping it with a cloth to remove any oil deposits.
Note: If the plug is oily, check around the plug hole to see if the oil is coming from outside or inside the hole. If the oil is from outside, check that the rocker box cover/cambox (cover at the top of the engine) is not leaking. If the leak is coming from inside the plug hole, check the condition of the sparplug's sealing washer.
• Use a stiff bristle sparkplug brush on the plug to clean the electrodes (Fig 121).

Fig 121. Cleaning with a sparkplug brush.

• Check that the sealing washer at the top of the sparkplug's threads is in good condition (Fig 115).

Setting the plug gap
You need to do this for new sparkplugs as well as for re-used sparkplugs.

• Use the feeler gauges, or all-in-one tool, to set the plug gap (Fig 122-123).
• The correct size gap can be found either in the car's handbook or on the internet. The gauge should just be able to slide between the electrodes when the gap is set to the correct size (Fig 124 and 125).

Fig 122. Set of feeler gauges.

Fig 122a. Thickness marked on each blade.

Fig 123.
All-in-one
sparkplug
tool.

Fig 124. Checking the gap between electrodes.

• If you do not have a setting tool, use a soft hammer to tap the outer electrode closed with the feeler gauge between the electrodes, checking all the time so as not to trap the gauge. If the gap needs to be increased, carefully ease the electrode away with a small pair of long-nosed pliers.

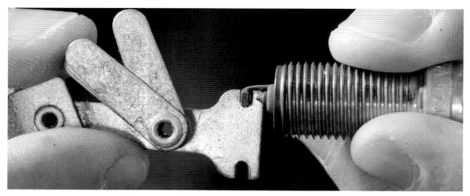

Fig 125. Adjusting the gap between electrodes.

Fitting

With the correct electrode gap set, the cleaned or new sparkplug can be fitted.
• Insert the plug into the plug socket, ensuring it's gripped by the grommet.

Spread a small amount of copper grease around the thread to help it screw in easily.

Note: Do not attach the ratchet at this stage, it's important that this part of refitting the plug is done by hand.
• Insert the plug into its hole and turn by hand only. If it's tight, remove the plug and try again, making sure it's at the right angle to enter the hole squarely. You should be able to screw the sparkplug in some way before it becomes too tight for you to turn by hand.

• When it's too tight for you to turn by hand, fit the ratchet.
• Hold the ratchet at the end above the socket, and continue to screw in the plug. Holding the ratchet in this way will help prevent you applying too much force.
• When the sparkplug is tight, use the handle end of the ratchet to turn the plug just a little further to lock it.
• Finally, remove the socket and refit the plug cap, ensuring that it's fully pushed onto the plug top.
• If you're fitting more than one sparkplug, repeat the same procedure for each.

six
Air filter

Fig 126. Different styles of air filter.

Note: Although important for petrol (gasoline) engines, a clean and efficient air filter is particularly important for diesel engines.

The air filter can be found under the bonnet, normally housed in a large plastic container, situated on or near the top of the engine – it's probably the biggest plastic component in the engine compartment, other than the plastic panel that may cover the engine itself.

Air filters come in many different shapes and sizes (Fig 126), but they all do the same job; filter the air before it enters the engine. The filter prevents dirt entering the engine because grit inside an engine can cause serious damage. So don't forget the air filter; it's a very important, but often overlooked, component.

Examination

The air filter housing is usually held closed by plastic clips or screws on either the top or end of the unit. Undo these clips/screws and either lift or slide the filter out of its housing.

The filter is usually made of pleated paper or foam held in a plastic surround. Check for holes and tears, which would mean that the filter must be renewed. Also renew the filter if it has been contaminated with oil, water, or is obviously dirty.

Clean or replace the filter?

A paper filter cannot be cleaned satisfactorily without causing damage to it, so immediate replacement is recommended.

If the filter is made of foam, and only slightly dirty, without holes or tears, then it can be cleaned by soaking in warm water and gently squeezing the water through. **Note:** Be aware that excessive squeezing can tear the inside of the filter, and that these tears may not be visible from the outside. If the filter is excessively dirty, renew it.

Fitting an air filter

Place the air filter in its holder. Check that it's in the correct position, and do up all the fastenings to secure it. Recheck all is seated correctly and close the bonnet fully.

Fig 127. Removing a typical air filter.

seven

Wipers, windscreen, & mirrors

Wipers

All wipers must be in good condition, and correctly attached to the wiper arm. Check the leading edge of the blade; it should be in one piece, without cuts or other damage, particularly at the ends (Fig 128). If the leading edge is damaged in any way, the wiper blade needs to be renewed.

There are several types of windscreen wiper blade fittings. The most common is where the wiper blade is fitted by pushing it into a curved mounting 'hook' at the end of the wiper arm.

To change a wiper blade

This procedure is for the most commonly found wiper blade/arm combinations.

• Pull the arm away from the windscreen until it locks into a position that holds it off the glass. The wiper

Fig 128. A damaged wiper blade.

blade is held against the windscreen by a spring (Fig 129) inside the wiper arm: this spring must be in good condition to maintain enough pressure on the blade to satisfactory clear water from the windscreen during heavy rain.

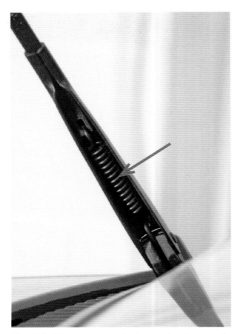

Fig 129. Wiper arm tensioning spring (arrowed).

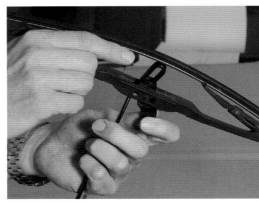

● To remove the blade, push the blade pivoting clip backward from the end of the arm to release the clip and blade from the U-shaped 'hook' at the end of the arm. Figs 130 & 131.

● The blade now needs to be threaded over the end of the arm to remove it completely.

● Your new blade may have the centre pivot clip as a separate item. If so, this needs to clipped into the blade as shown in Fig 132.

● With the centre pivot clipped in place, pass the end of the arm through the wiper blade and clip it fully into the 'hook' of the arm end. Place the wiper blade back against the windscreen.

● Another popular fitting type is where the wiper appears to be on the side of the arm. When the wiper arm is pulled away from the windscreen the blade can swivel on its pivot pin. The wiper

Figs 130 & 131. Removing the wiper blade from the arm. Fitting is the same procedure in reverse.

Fig 132. Fitting pivot clip to the wiper blade.

blade can be removed by rotating it
through 90 degrees and then pulling it
away from the arm and off the pivot pin.
• Wipers must park in the correct
position without obscuring the driver's
view. The most common position is
about 2.5cm to 5cm (1 to 2in) above the
base of the windscreen.

Windscreen

It's difficult to categorically state what
damage is acceptable, and what's not.
However, it would be foolish to drive a
car with vision obscured, even partially,
by a damaged windscreen.

In the UK, the main section of the
screen, as checked in the annual MoT
test, is an area on the driver's side of the
vehicle that is:
a: swept by the windscreen wiper
and
b: 290mm wide, centred on the middle
of the steering wheel
Chips in the windscreen (Fig 133)
can't be larger than 10mm in diameter
to pass the MoT and be repairable.
Chips that have been repaired, and are
virtually invisible, aren't a reason to fail
an MoT test.
If there's a chip anywhere in the
windscreen, it's recommended that you
get it repaired at the earliest opportunity.
Water ingress into the chip/crack can
freeze and cause the windscreen to
crack or crack further.
Cracks in the windscreen (Fig 134)
require the windscreen to be replaced.
There's no definition of a safe
cracked windscreen, and a police
officer can prohibit you from using your
car until the windscreen is replaced.
The main reason for this is that the
windscreen provides a good deal of the
body strength of the car.

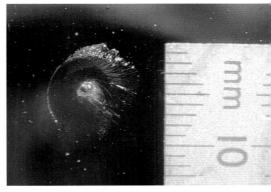

Fig 133. Chips like this should be repaired as a
matter of urgency. In the UK at least, this chip is
verging on the legal limit of 10mm.

Fig 134. This huge crack is dangerous and
beyond repair. This windscreen needs to be
replaced as a matter of urgency.

Mirrors

In the UK you are required by law to
have at least two mirrors that provide a
view to the rear of the vehicle. Mirrors
must be securely fitted and in good
condition (ie: not cracked or smashed).

eight

Battery, bulbs, & fuses

Battery

The battery is normally situated in the engine bay, and its primary function is to provide power to start your car. Car batteries vary in shape and size, with different types of connections. Normally the only maintenance needed for a car battery is the occasional top up with distilled water, unless it's a sealed type, in which case it will require only charging if it runs low or discharges completely.

Caution! A battery contains electrolyte (ie: acid), so be careful not to tip the battery over or spill its contents. Keep battery acid away from hands and eyes. If you come into contact with it, wash with copious amounts of clean, cold water. Medical attention will be required if battery acid comes into contact with the eyes.

Condition
If you do not check the battery on a

Fig 135. Two different car batteries – the one on the right is sealed and maintenance-free, the other isn't.

regular basis, it's likely to let you down when you least expect it. Do not ignore the battery, it's an integral part of your car's electrical system.

Identifying a problem with the battery

• Turn on the ignition. Does the ignition light glow steadily to show that you have electrical power? If the ignition light is dull or not lit at all, it's possible that there's a loose battery connection, or the battery itself requires attention.

• If when you try to start the engine it turns over slowly or not at all, it's another sign of possible battery problems.

Fig 138. Sealed battery (maintenance-free) in situ.

Checks & maintenance

• If there is a problem, first check that the power cables are tightly clamped to the terminal heads on the battery; a good connection can be helped by applying a small amount of petroleum jelly to the terminal heads.

• To visually check the battery you do not need to remove it from the car. Some batteries have an indicator built into the top that is green when the battery is in good condition, and red when it isn't (Figs 136 & 137).

• Do not attempt to open a sealed

Figs 136 & 137. Left: Sealed battery in poor condition (red); it will require charging or replacing. Right: Sealed battery in good condition (green).

Fig 139. Typical battery (not maintenance-free). Note the + (positive) and – (negative) symbols on the battery's body in front of the terminals (arrowed).

battery (Fig 138). No maintenance is required on a sealed battery other than keeping the connections in good condition.

Fig 140. Dry battery cells (no electrolyte above the plates).

Fig 141. Topping up the battery cells with distilled water.

the battery acid and lead to battery failure.

Checking the voltage

• With the ignition turned off and the key removed, ensure all other loads are turned off, such as interior lights, radio, etc, and connect a voltage meter (set to DC volts) to the battery (Fig 142). The voltage meter's BLACK lead goes to the (–) NEGATIVE terminal and the RED lead goes to the (+) POSITIVE terminal.

• The voltage shown on the meter should read about 12.4V or above for a 12 volt battery).

• If the battery is showing a low voltage, it will need to be charged.

• If the battery is not the sealed type, you can remove the cell plugs to see the level of electrolyte inside the battery (Fig 139). This electrolyte needs to be covering all the plates in each cell (Fig 140). If the fluid level is low, top it up (but do not overfill) with distilled water or battery top up fluid (Fig 141). Do not use tap water, as this will contaminate

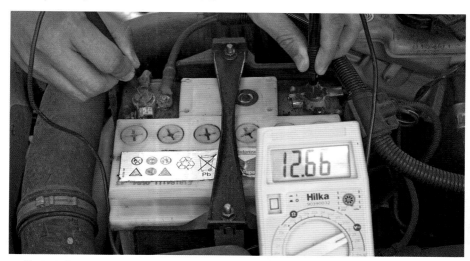

Fig 142. Checking battery voltage with a voltage meter. Reading shows a healthy 12.66 volts.

Charging the battery

- You do not need to remove the battery from the car, but ensure all loads, such as interior lights, radio, etc, are turned off, and that the ignition key is removed.
- Check that the correct amount of electrolyte is present in each cell (if the battery is not of the sealed type – see Fig 135), and top up if required.
- Ensure the car is in a well-ventillated space, so the fumes created during charging can easily disperse.
- Only use a battery charger designed to charge a car battery of corresponding voltage.

Fig 143a. Position the charger away from the battery if possible, and on a surface that can stand the small amount of heat generated by the charger.

Note: Never charge a car battery using a truck battery charger. These are likely to be 24V (too high) chargers, and will buckle the battery plates and render the battery useless.

- With the charger turned off, connect the RED cable from the charger to the (+) POSITIVE terminal on the battery, and the BLACK cable to the (–) NEGATIVE terminal (Fig 143).

Pay particular attention to the instructions that came with the battery charger (Fig 144), as it's possible to cause damage to the battery by overcharging.

- Loosen the battery cell filler caps (if fitted).

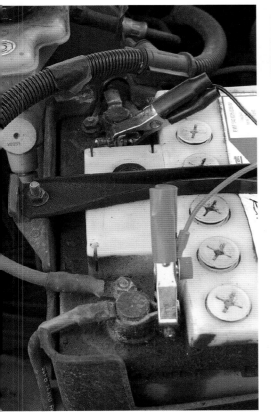

Fig 143. Charger connections at battery. Note loosened cell filler caps.

75

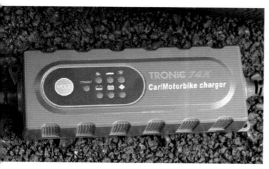

Fig 144. Some multi-purpose chargers need to be set to a specific purpose; charging a car battery in this instance.

• Check that the charger is set to the correct voltage, then turn it on.
• When the battery has fully charged, which might take several hours, turn off the battery charger before disconnecting the cables from the battery (negative first) and tightening the cell caps.

Removing the battery

If you need to remove the battery from the vehicle for any reason, carry out the following:

• First check that you have access to the immobiliser and radio codes, which may be required once the battery has been reinstalled as these items need to be reset.
• Ensure that the engine and ignition has been turned off for about 10-15min (to allow the Electronic Control Unit to power down), and that the ignition key is removed.
• Remove the battery cover (if fitted). Then completely disconnect the (–) NEGATIVE terminal first, by loosening the clamp nut, and moving the terminal clamp and cable away from the terminal. Then disconnect the (+) POSITIVE terminal.
• Undo any battery securing straps or brackets. **Note:** There must be a means

of securing the battery; an unsecured battery is unsafe, and is an MoT test failure in the UK.
• You can now remove the battery from the car – use the battery handle (if fitted). **Caution!** Car batteries are heavy, so be careful – don't drop it!

Refitting the battery

• Lift the battery into its correct position in the car (ensuring it's the right way round and no cables are trapped) and refit the securing straps or brackets.
• Protect the battery pillars from corrosion and aid a good power connection by smearing a small amount of 'Vaseline' or other form of petroleum jelly over the terminal pillars before connecting the cables.
• Connect the RED cable to the (+) POSITIVE terminal on the battery first, ensuring that the terminal is clean. Check that the cable is attached firmly.
• Now connect the BLACK cable to the (–) NEGATIVE terminal in the same way.

Checking the charging system

It's possible to do a quick check on the car's charging system by connecting a voltage meter to the battery installed in the car.

• Set the meter to DC volts.
• Connect the red (+) terminal/wire on the meter to the red (+) terminal on the battery, then the black (–) terminal/wire on the meter to the black (–) terminal on the battery.
• Start the engine.
• The voltage meter should show a voltage increase as the engine is revved slightly; about 13.5-14.5V for a 12V system (Fig 145). You should be able to position the voltage meter so that you can read it (eg: through the windscreen) as you rev the engine, but you may find it easier to ask someone to help.

If there's no change in voltage, the

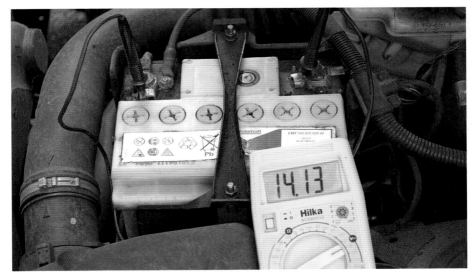

Fig145. Volt meter showing a 14.13 volt charge with the engine running.

charging system needs to be checked, a process which is outside the scope of this book.

If you've followed all the instructions in this section and the condition of the battery hasn't improved, get it checked by a garage, which will use professional equipment to test the condition of the battery and determine if it requires replacement.

Bulbs

It's important to regularly check that all your car's lights are working. It's unsafe, as well as illegal, to drive with defective lights.

Changing a headlight bulb

Note: It can be possible to upgrade your headlight bulbs by installing higher wattage versions than those originally fitted by the manufacturer, but be aware that higher wattage means

higher temperatures. Most headlight units are made from plastic, so the use of higher wattage bulbs could cause them to become misshapen because of the extra heat. It's best to contact the vehicle manufacturer for advice if you are interested in upgrading.

Fig 146. A range of bulb types.

HID headlight bulbs

Figs 147 & 148. Some manufacturers are now fitting as standard, 'Xenon'/HID (High intensity discharge) lighting systems (your handbook will tell you if your car is so equipped). HID units provide up to 300 per cent more light than some ordinary bulbs and consume less electricity.

Unlike ordinary bulbs, HID bulbs do not have a regular metal filament. They work on the principle of a spark of around 20,000 volts being used to activate the gas and metal salts contained in a tube to form a plasma, then a continuous supply of around 85 volts is required to keep the arc lit.

If you have these bulbs fitted, they generally give a warning when they are about to fail, in that they may start to flicker.

It is not recommended that you change these bulbs yourself, mainly because the high voltages required to operate them represent a real hazard if the lights are not completely isolated electrically. HID bulbs are very expensive and easily damaged, and it is also easily possible that the fault is in the electrical equipment supporting the HID units, rather than the bulbs themselves.

It is recommended that you use a local auto electrical technician to investigate any problems with HID headlights.

Fig 147. If your car has very small headlights within the headlight housing, they are likely to be HID units, as here (your handbook will confirm).

Fig 148. An electrical danger sticker like this on the back of the headlight unit indicates that HID bulbs are employed.

Removing the old bulb (non-HID)

• Open the bonnet (hood) and locate the rear of the headlight unit.

• Open the headlight bulb access panel (if fitted), as shown in Fig 149. It may be held by:

1) A spring clip that goes across the back of the panel – the clip is pulled up from the back of the panel thereby allowing the panel to be removed.

2) A plastic clip that needs to be pushed down to release the back panel.

3) A plug in a rubber holder.

• Locate the rear of the bulb that needs replacing and remove its wiring connector – pull the connector off, don't try to remove it by pulling the wires; also try not to twist the connector as you pull it (Fig 150).

Note: The connector may have two or three wires attached to it, depending on the bulb type (ie: full beam and dipped beam in one bulb or two separate bulbs).

• The bulb itself is held in place by a spring clip over the back, which has one

Fig 149. Opening the headlight access panel at the back of the headlight.

Fig 151. Close-up of a typical wire clip bulb holder. To release the bulb the non-pivoting end of the clip is pushed inward and then slid to the left to release the clip and the bulb.

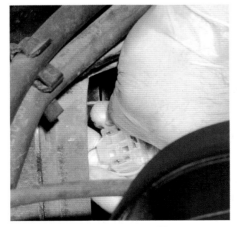

Fig 150. Removing the bulb's wiring connector by pulling it off the rear of the bulb.

or two small lugs (generally at the top). Push the two lugs together, or push the single lug to one side, and slightly forwards, to release the spring clip so that it comes away from the back of the bulb – the clip will swivel to the side or downward so that the bulb can be removed through the back of the headlight unit.

• Take out the bulb, holding it – if possible – the way it came out of the

Fig 152. Removing the bulb whilst keeping it in the same orientation.

Fig 153. The base of the bulb shows the spade-type terminals which slot into the connector.

unit, as this gives you an idea of how to correctly seat the new bulb (Fig 152).
• Still holding the bulb as you removed it, note its orientation and examine the base closely – there will be indentations and/or mounting lugs on the bulb fitting that you'll have to locate in the same positions to correctly fit the new bulb (Fig 153).

Fitting the new bulb (non-HID)
• Take the new bulb from its packaging. **Note:** Do not touch the glass with your fingers, as the natural oils in your skin will burn onto the lamp glass when it's first used, and reduce bulb brightness. If there isn't a piece of foam around the bulb, handle it with a double layer of tissue.
• Fit the new bulb into its recess in the same orientation as the old bulb.
• Bring the spring clip over the back of the bulb, ensuring that both the clip and bulb are seated correctly; the holding clip will clip into the correct position when pushed forward against the back of the bulb.
• Reattach the wiring connector and test the bulb.
• Replace the panel and fit the securing clip over the back of it.
• Check that the access panel is secure, and close the bonnet.

If your car has separate high and low beam bulbs, they can either both be found in the same unit or in separate units. The method for accessing and removing them is usually the same as previously described.

Side lights & front turn indicators
These lights can be in the same cluster or in separate ones, and the bulbs usually push and twist-fit into a rubber/plastic mount.

Some cars will have bulb holders at the rear of the light cluster. To change a bulb in this type of fitting, push in the holder slightly and twist anti-clockwise to remove holder and bulb as one. Push the bulb into the holder and twist to remove it. Replace the bulb with a new one of the same type and wattage, and refit.

Sometimes side lights and/or turn indicator bulbs can be accessed either from the front by undoing the screw or screws retaining the lens, or from the rear, which may give direct access to the holder itself, in which case you simply twist the bulbs anti-clockwise to remove.

Rear light clusters

It's imperative that bulbs in rear light clusters are replaced like-for-like, as each will have a certain wattage, depending on its purpose. You will find the wattage marked on the old bulb or, if in doubt, in the handbook.

Access to the rear of the cluster is normally via a panel inside the rear of the car (Fig 154 and 155), or by removing the complete light cluster from the outside of the car (Fig 156 and 157).

The access panel may be held closed by clips, screws or even velcro. Once you have access to the bulbs or bulb holders, push the relevant holder in slightly and twist anti-clockwise to remove it – the bulb and holder come out as one (Fig 157). Push the bulb into the holder and twist to remove it. If there are no holders (as in Fig 155) simply push and twist the bulbs to remove.

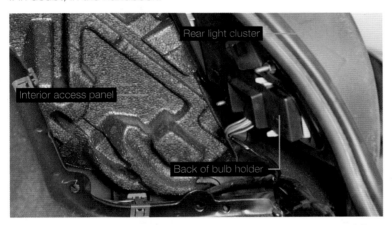

Fig 154. Access to the bulbs in this typical rear light cluster is from the interior luggage area. The panel inside the car is pulled back to reveal the back of the bulb holder.

Fig 155. The bulb holder is pulled away from the rear light cluster, bringing the bulbs with it so that one or more can be replaced.

81

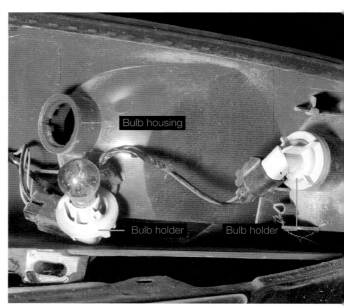

Bulb housing

Bulb holder

Bulb holder

Fig 156. This typical rear light cluster is released from the car's body as a complete unit by undoing a single retaining screw (arrowed). This done, the rear of the unit can be accessed as shown in the next photo.

Fig 157. The back of the cluster reveals the bulb holders. The bulb holder/bulb to the left has been removed from the bulb housing by twisting the holder anti-clockwise.

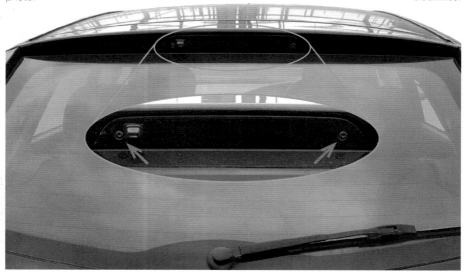

Fig 158. A typical high-level brake light with two external fixing screws.

High-level brake lights

Access is generally by removing a small panel directly behind the unit, or the lens is removed by undoing two screws from the outside (Fig 158).

These lights are normally formed from a number of LEDs. Depending on the manufacturer, these can either be changed one LED at a time, or only as a whole new unit.

Fuses

Fuses are used to protect electrical circuits from too high amperage, thereby preventing damage or even fire in the electronics of the car.

Caution! It's essential that any 'blown' fuse is replaced with one of the same type and size. If its not possible to see visual evidence that the fuse has blown (its filament is broken/missing) then you test it using a multimeter that has a continuity test facility or, simply, try a new fuse.

Fusebox

The fusebox (Fig 159) can be located in almost any accessible position in the car, but is often in the engine compartment, in the boot (trunk) or inside the car, below the dashboard, on the driver or passenger side. The vehicle handbook will tell you where your car's fusebox is and whether there is more than one fusebox.

Although it's called a 'fusebox' it may well contain other items like headlight and/or indicator relays, but in this book we are concerned only with the fuses themselves.

You may find a key to the fuse positions/functions on the lid of the fusebox or on the inside of the lid. If not, consult the car's handbook.

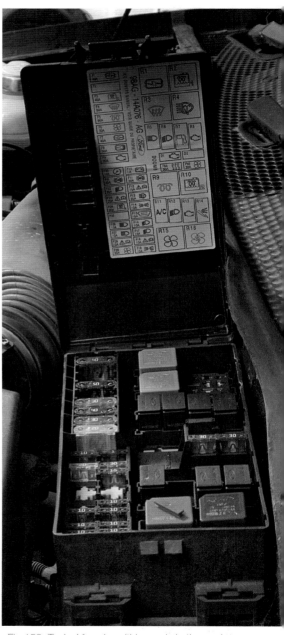

Fig 159. Typical fuse box (this one is in the engine compartment). The lid is secured by clips.

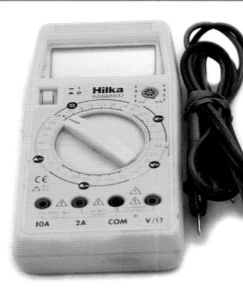

Fig 160. A typical multimeter.

profile mini, mini, regular and maxi. Whatever the fuse size, the insulator colour always relates to the amperage. Maxi have a different amp range for the same colours as they cover higher rate circuits.

Fig 161.
Blade fuses.

The top of the box is usually held closed by clips, or sometimes screws.

If your car has more than one fusebox only one of these will be the main fuse box. Other fuseboxes are normally for specific electrical circuits that aren't user serviceable.

It's usually easy to tell if a fuse has blown or not just by looking at it, but you can use a multimeter (Fig 160) to check for a complete circuit through the fuse if you are unsure, or simply fit a new fuse to see if it cures the problem.

Types of fuse
Fuses come in different shapes, sizes and ratings. Only replace a fuse with one of the same design and rating (marked on the fuse). **Caution!** Using a higher rated fuse than required could lead to overheating of the wires and cause a fire.

Blade fuses
Pretty much universal nowadays, blade fuses come in four different sizes: low-

	Low-profile mini, mini & regular	Maxi
Dark blue	0.5	
Black	1	
Gray	2	25
Voilet	3	100
Pink	4	
Tan	5	70
Brown	7.5	
Red	10	50
Blue	15	60
Yellow	20	20
Clear	25	80
Green	30	30
Blue green		35
Orange	40	40
Brown		35
Purple		120

Replacing a fuse
The method for replacing the different fuse types is described below. Always begin by ensuring the ignition is turned off and that the key is removed.

If after replacing the fuse the same electrical problem exists, you need to check for blown bulbs, chafed/broken wires, etc, depending on what the main problem is. Some problems will be beyond your capabilities and will require an auto-electric technician to fix.

Blade fuse

There is usually a selection of spare fuses inside the fusebox. If you use one of these spares, it's in your best interest to replace it as soon as possible.

A fuse removal tool can usually be found in fuse boxes: it looks like a short pair of plastic tweezers. Grip the fuse between the jaws of the tool and pull it out to remove. Replacement is the reverse procedure (Fig 162).

If the removal tool is missing, you could try using your fingers, but a small pair of long-nosed pliers is the best option (but only grip the plastic fuse top).

Fig 162. Replacing a spade fuse using the tool usually found in the fusebox.

nine
Safety checks

This chapter lists most items covered by the annual MoT test in the UK, and outlines what the inspector is looking for (orange text). However, regardless of the country you live in, it's very much in your interest to regularly check the condition/operation of these items.

Lights
All must be in working order.
Front side lights
Headlight high and low beam
Headlight aim
Must be within the correct hight range and angled so as not to blind oncoming traffic.
Rear number (licence) plate lights
Rear foglight/s (if fitted)
Stoplights
Direction (turn) indicators
Hazard warning lights
Reversing lights
Rear reflectors

Steering & suspension
Steering control
Excessive play (lash) at the steering wheel, steering wheel loose.
Steering system
Excessive play in trackrod end ball joints, and any other joints.
Power steering (if fitted)
Must work effectively.
Suspension
Broken springs, rusted mountings.
Front wheel bearings
Excessive play on bearings.
Driveshafts
Loose driveshafts, split CV boots.
Shock absorbers
Ineffective, leaking oil.

Brakes
Handbrake/parking brake lever
Loose or ineffective.
Hand-operated brake control valves
Work correctly where fitted.
Handbrake operation
Ineffective or frayed cables.

Anti-lock braking system
Ineffective.
Mechanical brake components
Failed or seized parts.
Hydraulic, air, and vacuum systems
Ineffective, leaking, or severely
corroded.
Brake performance
All wheels must brake according to the
stated test criteria.

Driving
Drivers view of the road
Cracks, chips or anything that will
obscure the drivers view.
Windscreen
(As above)
Wipers
Must clean the screen satisfactory.
Washers
Must work and deliver water to the
correct area.
Horn
Must work.
Seatbelts
Must work correctly.

Exhaust
Exhaust system
Must be in a satisfactory condition
without leaks.
Exhaust emissions: petrol & diesel
Must meet the stated test criteria.

Bodywork
Vehicle structure
Is the body sound, without damage that

may injure a pedestrian?
Body security
Is the body secure on the chassis?
Body condition
No serious rust in structural, load
bearing areas.
Doors
Are they fully secured to the vehicle
when opened and closed?
Load security
Are the doors or boot likely to come
open when in motion?
Spare wheel and carrier
Is the spare wheel legal and securely
fastened?
Seats
Are they working in satisfactory
condition, and mounted securely?
Mirrors
Must be intact, and at least two mirrors
should be fitted.

Other
Tyres
Worn or other defect.
Road wheels
Damaged rims or other defect.
Fuel system
Is the fuel system leaking or are fumes
getting into the vehicle?
Registration (licence) plates
Are they legal, and is the style and
spacing of lettering correct?
VIN details
Do the details match the vehicle?
Battery
Must be secured to the vehicle.

RƎC
the driving people

How your car works

Your guide to the components
& systems of modern cars,
including hybrid & electric
vehicles

Arvid Linde

ISBN: 978-1-845843-90-8
• Paperback • 21x14.8cm • £12.99* UK/$24.95* USA
• 128 pages • 92 colour and b&w pictures

For more info on Veloce titles, visit our website at www.veloce.co.uk
• email: info@veloce.co.uk • Tel: +44(0)1305 260068
* prices subject to change, p&p extra

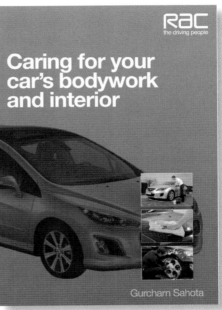

ISBN: 978-1-845840-95-2
• Paperback • 21x14.8cm • £9.99*
UK/$19.95* USA • 80 pages
• 101 colour pictures

Aimed at the rider who wants to do his or her own basic scooter maintenance and servicing without the need for in-depth mechanical knowledge, or a technical manual. A must-have for scooter users.

ISBN: 978-1-845843-88-5
• Paperback • 21x14.8cm • £9.99*
UK/$19.95* USA • 80 pages
• 110 pictures

A clean and well-tended car will look better, be more pleasurable to drive, and have a superior resale value. This book is a step-by-step guide to the various elements of car care, from washing, waxing and polishing to engine cleaning and leather maintenance.

For more info on Veloce titles, visit our website at www.veloce.co.uk
• email: info@veloce.co.uk • Tel: +44(0)1305 260068
* prices subject to change, p&p extra

Also from Veloce Publishing –

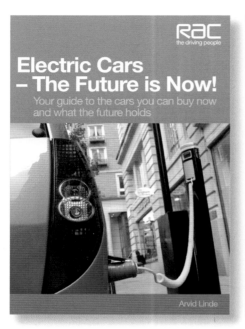

ISBN: 978-1-845843-10-6
• Paperback • 21x14.8cm • £12.99*
UK/$24.95* USA • 128 pages
• 67 colour and b&w pictures

ISBN: 978-1-845843-51-9
• Paperback • 21x14.8cm • £9.99*
UK/$19.95* USA • 96 pages
• 32 colour pictures

What if we all had to say goodbye to
petrol cars tomorrow? Would you be
ready? This book will help you find out.
With a concise catalogue covering the
best production models and the most
promising prototypes, this book is the
definitive guide to the future of motoring.

Describes in a clear, friendly manner
everything today's driver needs to know
about choosing and using a car in
an economical and eco-efficient way.
Includes helpful information on alternative
fuels, hybrid powertrains, and much more.

For more info on Veloce titles, visit our website at www.veloce.co.uk
• email: info@veloce.co.uk • Tel: +44(0)1305 260068
* prices subject to change, p&p extra

ISBN: 978-1-845841-02-7
• Paperback • 15x10.5cm • £4.99* UK/$9.95* USA
• 208 pages • 200 colour pictures

Anyone who drives on the motorways will benefit from this
guide to walks within 5 miles of motorway exits. All of the UK is
covered, from Exeter to Perth, and Swansea to Canterbury.

For more info on Veloce titles, visit our website at www.veloce.co.uk
• email: info@veloce.co.uk • Tel: +44(0)1305 260068
* prices subject to change, p&p extra

Roads with a View is not just another travel guide series. These books have been written by a driver especially for fellow motorists, and provide detailed accounts of the best English, Welsh, and Scottish roads to drive on, and the best places to drive to for that stunning front seat view. Features specially drawn maps, beautiful colour photography, and plenty of travel advice.

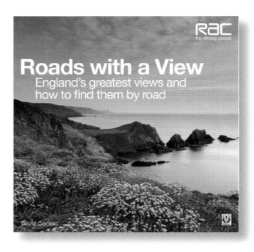

ISBN: 978-1-845843-50-2
• Hardback • 25x25cm • £19.99* UK/$45.00* USA • 144 pages
• 57 colour and b&w pictures

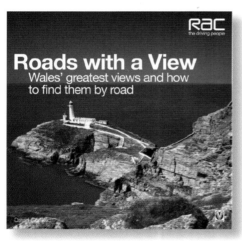

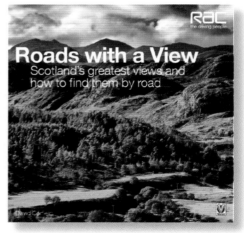

ISBN: 978-1-845843-67-0
• Hardback • 25x25cm • £19.99* UK/$45.00* USA • 144 pages
• 57 pictures

ISBN: 978-1-845843-68-7
• Hardback • 25x25cm • £19.99* UK/$45.00* USA • 144 pages
• 57 pictures

For more info on Veloce titles, visit our website at www.veloce.co.uk
• email: info@veloce.co.uk • Tel: +44(0)1305 260068
* prices subject to change, p&p extra

Index

VISIT VELOCE ON THE WEB – WWW.VELOCE.CO.UK
All current books • New book news • Special offers • Gift vouchers • Forum